Hannah Nunn

Illuminate

Contemporary Craft Lighting

First published in Great Britain in 2012
A & C Black Publishers Limited
an imprint of Bloomsbury Publishing Plc
50 Bedford Square
London WC1B 3DP
www.acblack.com

ISBN: 978-1-408-14704-7

CIP Catalogue records for this book are available from the British Library.

Typeset in Akkurat Light Pro
Book design by Evelin Kasikov
Cover design by Sutchinda Thompson
Printed and bound in China

This book is produced using paper that is made from wood grown in managed, sustainable forests. It is natural, renewable and recyclable. The logging and manufacturing processes conform to the environmental regulations of the country of origin.

Cover image: Zipper 8 Lighting, *Spiky White Paper Pendant Light.* Pendant light constructed from hundreds of hand-cut white vellum paper triangles, 50.8 x 45.7 x 45.7 cm (20 x 18 x 18 in.). *Photo: Allison Patrick.*

Title page image: Curiousa & Curiousa, *Glass Pendants*. Bespoke, mouth-blown glass pendants. Height from 12 to 16 cm (4¾ to 6¼ in.). *Photo: Chris Webb.*

Hannah Nunn

Illuminate

Contemporary Craft Lighting

B L O O M S B U R Y
LONDON • NEW DELHI • NEW YORK • SYDNEY

CONTENTS

SARAH FOOTE, *HYDRANGEA LAMP*.
From afar, the *Hydrangea Lamp* looks like dozens of small branches grouped into a bouquet, 35.5 x 35.5 x 40.5 cm (14 x 14 x 16 in.). *Photo: Kate Sears.*

7 About the author
8 Acknowledgements
10 Introduction

1

12 **CERAMICS**

14 Liz Emtage
16 Amy Cooper
18 Holly Ross
20 Perch!
23 Scabetti

2

26 **TEXTILES**

28 Rachel O'Neill
30 Ai Kawauchi
32 Ana Kraš
34 Maartje van den Noort
37 Maxine Sutton
40 Isabel Stanley

3

42 **PAPER**

44 Hannah Nunn
47 Andrew Ooi
50 Louise Traill
52 Celine Wright
54 HiiH Lights

4

56 **PRINT**

58 Lush Designs
60 Helen Minns
62 House of Chintz
65 De Maria's
68 Helen Rawlinson
70 Laura Slater
72 Daniel O'Riordan

5

74 **WOOD**

76 Jane Blease
79 Tom Raffield
82 David Trubridge
84 Sarah Lock
86 Sarah Foote

6

88 **METAL**

90 Chris Cain
92 Lightexture
94 Colin Chetwood
97 Emerald Faerie
100 David Wiseman

7

102 **GLASS**

104 Aline Johnson
107 Rothschild & Bickers
110 Curiousa & Curiousa
113 Heather Gillespie
116 Penelope Batley

8

118 **RECYCLED MATERIALS**

120 Graypants
123 Umbu Lumière
126 Lucentia
128 Michelle Brand
130 Sarah Turner

132 Gallery
142 Websites
144 Index

About the author

Hannah Nunn runs a successful practice as a designer and maker of paper-cut lighting. She sells her work widely in the UK and across the world through many craft galleries and interior design shops. Her lighting has appeared in national publications such as *BBC Homes & Antiques*, *The Times* and *The Guardian Gift Guide* and has featured on blogs such as *Design Sponge* and *Apartment Therapy*. This coverage, along with her website and Etsy shop, has helped her build a customer base across the globe.

Her own practice as a lighting designer sparked a passion for handmade lighting and in 2005 Hannah opened her shop Radiance in Hebden Bridge, Yorkshire, to showcase some of the exceptional makers using light to bring their craft to life. She has her design studio at the back of the premises and enjoys the balance between sourcing and making beautiful work for the shop. Hannah has always loved to tell the stories behind the designs. Writing *Illuminate* has given her the opportunity to do just that and further champion the work of many designers working in the field.

Hannah lives in Hebden Bridge with her partner, two children and three cats.

ABOVE
The author, Hannah Nunn.
Photo: Sarah Mason.

LEFT
Hannah Nunn's fairy lights in the Radiance shop at night.
Photo: John Siddique.

Acknowledgements

I would like to thank you – Robert, Ffion, Euan, Rachel, Natalie, Wendy, Anne, Fiona, Matthew, Cathy and Rachel – in a big way for all your encouragement and support during the time I have been compiling this book. I love you all and couldn't have done this without you. Special thanks to Ffion for taking the time to help me.

Thanks to Alison Hawkes who had the vision for the book and offered me the opportunity and to Kate Sherington for her patience and support in seeing it through.

Thank you to all my wonderful customers who have helped my business to flourish. I wouldn't be here without you and for that I am grateful.

A huge thanks also to all the designers in the book. It has been a great honour to get to know you. Your time and effort is much appreciated; without your beautiful lights this book would not exist.

Lastly, Mum and Dad: you have always encouraged me to follow my heart and do what I love, and for that I can't thank you enough.

GRAYPANTS, *SCRAP LIGHTS – JUPITER WITH MOONS.*
Spherical series of repurposed cardboard pendants. Spheres ranging from 20–44.5 cm diameter (8–17½ in.).
Photo: Jonathan Junker.

1

2

Introduction

This is a book of stories. It captures 47 'light-bulb moments', telling the tales of many designers, ceramicists, furniture designers, blacksmiths and illustrators, all of whom were going about their business when one day something happened: they discovered light. In their different ways, they witnessed just how light could affect the work they were creating and they couldn't help but explore its properties in greater depth.

I am often asked, 'Have you always wanted to be a lighting designer?'

The answer is no! I hadn't considered this as a career path or that such a career even existed. I am an artist who happened upon light one day. I saw how well it enhanced my work and so invited it to come along for the journey. It seems to be a similar story throughout this book.

Illuminate tells the tales of many happy accidents. It recalls what happens when something nudges us to hold up our paper-cutting, our wood-shaving or our plastic-bottle end to the light. These are the golden moments (as eco-lighting designer Michelle Brand puts it) that have filled us with inspiration and taken us down the career path of designing with light.

And what was the great attraction? What was it that we couldn't ignore? In different ways, everyone describes a similar thing. The work was brought to life, animated, transformed. The light added another dimension, gave the work a personality, added magic. People discovered that it revealed hidden qualities in materials, like looking through a microscope at something.

The lights you will see in this book are essentially art and craft pieces. The work has been made for the love of the craft itself. This is not mass-produced design and many of the makers featured here are not particularly interested in getting their work made on a large scale. They would rather roll up their sleeves and get their hands dirty. It's about loving clay or wood. It's about loving print or stitch, or making something beautiful out of waste materials. For some, the work comes from a passion to keep a traditional technique alive; for others, it's paving the way for state-of-the-art technology to become a part of the craft world. Whatever the pull, each piece reflects this passion and embodies the warmth of human touch.

Many of the makers specialise in one craft but often delve into other mediums too. I have divided the book into eight chapters, each representing a different medium, but you will notice there are many crossovers. Where do I put a blacksmith who adorns his copper lamp bases with paper flower shades? Does someone making lampshades from old sewing patterns fit into 'paper' or 'recycled materials'? Please take my classifications lightly. Remember that what links together everyone in the book is light itself.

I find the creations in this book to be astonishingly beautiful, innovative and inspiring. The lighting these designers have made is full of artistry and immense creativity. It has been a great joy to talk to everyone about what they do and to hear all the fascinating stories of how their lighting came to be. Now, let there be light!

1
HANNAH NUNN AT WORK.
Photo: Ffion Atkinson.

2
HANNAH NUNN'S FLOWERING RUSH DESIGN, ABOUT TO BE CUT.
Photo: Hannah Nunn.

3
ARTIST HELEN RAWLINSON PULLING A SCREEN-PRINT.
Photo: courtesy of the artist.

3

1 CERAMICS

This chapter profiles five ceramic artists who have all embraced the many potentials of working with clay and light. In my research, I found many great ceramicists making lighting, more than in any other medium. Perhaps this is because clay allows the designer/maker endless scope for creating sculptural shapes and forms and exploring surface texture. The translucent qualities of porcelain and bone china invite themselves to be lit up, allowing the light to permeate right through the clay. An opaque clay body makes for a very different effect; impenetrable, it invites a dramatic contrast between the clay itself and the cut-out shapes through which the light escapes.

Clay can take on many colours and textures. It can be highly decorated or remain earthy and natural. It can be used to create indoor lighting, both decorative and practical, but is also robust enough to withstand the outdoors. The possibilities for design and use are endless, and mould-making and casting give ceramic artists another advantage, allowing them to reproduce their pieces simply and consistently.

The end result is something solid and permanent, which, if handled with the love and care it deserves, can last for many years.

1
AMY COOPER, *SMALL NAKED URCHIN LAMP.*
Porcelain lamp, 9 x 12 x 9 cm (3½ x 4¾ x 3½ in.). *Photo: Amy Cooper.*

Liz Emtage

UNITED KINGDOM

1
LIZ EMTAGE, *ALPSTEIN LAMP.*
Large porcelain lamp decorated with glaze stains, based on a view of the Austrian Alps, 48 x 16 x 16 cm (19 x 6¼ x 6¼ in.). *Photo: Sussie Ahlburg.*

2
LIZ EMTAGE, *ROSES TEA LIGHT.*
Pink porcelain tealight impressed with roses, 13 x 10 x 10 cm (5 x 4 x 4 in.). *Photo: Sussie Ahlburg.*

3
LIZ EMTAGE, *EXTRA-LARGE AQUA GRASS LAMP, EXTRA-LARGE RED RICE LAMP AND LARGE FLYING GRASSES LAMP.*
Group of porcelain lamps, extra-large: 54 x 20 x 20 cm (21¼ x 8 x 8 in.), large: 48 x 16 x 16 cm (19 x 6¼ x 6¼ in.). *Photo: Sussie Ahlburg.*

Ceramic artist Liz Emtage started working with light around 15 years ago when she was asked by a friend to make a ceramic light box. Reluctant at first, she set about playing with paperclay and soon realised just how well it worked with light. This paved the way for a whole ceramic lighting collection spanning table lamps, wall lamps, tea-light holders and large architectural lampshades, which she creates in her studio at Cockpit Arts in London.

Liz handbuilds her forms using large, rolled slabs of clay. She then embeds objects such as leaves and petals into the clay and, when fired, the organic material burns out in the kiln leaving a shape or pattern behind that is beautifully enhanced by lighting the lamp. Her main inspiration comes from plants and flowers – her lamps feature summer grasses, honesty seeds and cow-parsley heads, to name a few – but she also uses a variety of foodstuffs, such as rice and spaghetti, to great effect.

Each lamp holds a story – perhaps of a summer walk down a favourite Norfolk country lane, or of a special time. Liz has even made lamps using the flowers from her wedding bouquets, a unique way to preserve special memories.

Liz makes her paperclay by mixing porcelain with paper pulp. The paper fibres not only strengthen the clay, but the porcelain's already translucent qualities are enhanced when the paper is burned away in the kiln. Sometimes she mixes glaze into the clay body so that the whole lamp glows a soft green or blue, or she adds glaze afterwards to highlight particular details.

Liz has always been influenced by light. She loves bright sunny days and the warmth of firelight – not just the physical warmth but the emotional warmth and the comfort that it brings. Being able to light up the work she has created and imbue someone's home with this feeling brings her happiness.

1

3

2

Amy Cooper

UNITED KINGDOM

1

'Light for me is a very emotive medium.'

— **AMY COOPER**

Amy Cooper creates delicate porcelain forms, which, when lit, reveal exquisite texture and intriguing detail. It is easy to see that she's been inspired by the sea. Her glowing *Urchins* and *Sand Dollars* are a beautiful expression of the many childhood hours she spent playing in rock pools in Cornwall, where she grew up. She is also inspired by many other facets of the natural world, from the microscopic – pollen, seeds and spores – to nature on a much grander scale – meteors, glaciers and icebergs. In more recent work she has been moved by her immediate surroundings, like the magic of a woodland at twilight or dawn, as well as half-remembered animations from her childhood.

Amy first had the idea to make lights while studying at Wolverhampton University. Spending a lot of time projecting slide images on to different forms, she became obsessed with how light can transform an object from mundane to intriguing. 'It was quite literally a light-bulb moment as I wondered how the carved porcelain would look with a light through it,' she says. 'I was immediately convinced.' This obsession has stayed with her as she continues to develop her collection of beautiful lighting.

After living in Brighton and Devon she has now settled back in Cornwall and works from a studio overlooking her garden at the back of her house. 'Having the studio at home is invaluable since, having children, it means I can seize and utilise any free moments as they become available,' she says.

There are many processes involved in making a lamp. The pieces are slip-moulded in porcelain. Amy casts them quickly so that they are very thin and then decorates each one with slips and glazes when they are fresh out of the mould. Particular tools become indispensable for creating texture and detail, such as the wooden skewer she uses for piercing the clay or the end of a particular paintbrush with which she makes dents and bumps.

2

The pieces are then given a bisque firing, which increases their strength, and so allows her to sand each piece to achieve a flawless finish. She applies glaze by spraying so that she can control and vary the finish. Then it's left to dry and fired again, this time to 1250°C (2282°F). Unglazed work is polished with a diamond pad for an enticingly smooth finish. Her more recent pieces, such as *Hazel Saplings* and *Peacock Feathers*, are created by gluing on a template from a drawing and sandblasting until the areas that are covered by the stencil stand out.

'Light for me is a very emotive medium,' Amy says. 'It has the quality of creating an atmosphere or transforming a mood, but it can also suggest energy, warmth and life.' When lighting a piece for the first time, the moment of transformation still holds the same allure for her that it did when she lit her first lamp over ten years ago.

1
AMY COOPER, *GREATER SPOTTED FAT POLLEN.*
Porcelain lamp, diameter approx. 12 cm (4¾ in.). *Photo: Fotofit.*

2
AMY COOPER, *HAZEL SAPLINGS.*
Porcelain lamp with sandblasted imagery, 35 x 10 x 10 cm (13¾ x 4 x 4 in.). *Photo: Amy Cooper.*

Holly Ross

UNITED KINGDOM

'It's almost like my work and the light itself have merged together as one. I couldn't think of not having light now.'

— HOLLY ROSS

1

Holly Ross's *Wonderland Wonders* collection came about during her final year at Bournemouth University where she was studying ceramics. 'I was inspired by a lot of things all at once,' she says, 'and the idea evolved from basic shapes into pieces with a world of their own.' Islamic architecture led her to experiment with a range of pointed domed shapes, finally leading to the forms for her birdcages and houses. Exploring the translucent qualities of fine bone china then led her to experiment with light, and reading fairy tales and children's stories brought the inspiration for her illustrative elements.

The forms are cast with fine bone-china slip in a plaster mould and left to harden overnight. Then she uses piercing, carving, shellac resist and imprinting to create surface texture. After a week of drying Holly can start the firing process. There are three firings altogether: the original firing, a second firing where she applies oxides and translucent glaze, and finally the print firing. Holly found that print gave a whole new dimension to her work. The light defined the black, blocked-out image and she was immediately enchanted by the mysterious, shadowy silhouettes created.

Her idea to use chain came simply from the hanging of birdcages. Holly found that the contrast between the light airiness of the bone china and the darkness of the chain was alluring and that the final added jewel gave a burst of colour and added a twinkling charm.

Holly stands her ceramic pieces on white wooden plinths, which house the electrics. She uses a very low-wattage LED bulb which doesn't create heat inside her closed ceramic forms. Holly says, 'It's almost like my work and the light itself have merged together as one. I couldn't think of not having light now.' There are so many intricate details in Holly's work and each one is revealed when the light is switched on. It is a truly magical combination.

1
HOLLY ROSS, *WONDERLAND WONDERS HOUSE.*
Bone-china house lamp. 26 x 12¾ x 12¾ cm (10¼ x 5 x 5 in.). *Photo: Holly Ross.*

2
HOLLY ROSS, *WONDERLAND WONDERS COLLECTION.*
A collection of bone-china birdcage lamps, all approx, 20 x 13 x 13 cm (8 x 5 x 5 in.). *Photo: courtesy of the artist.*

2

Perch!

UNITED STATES

'I think as designers we are good at seeing the potential in materials and taking things out of context, so I was willing to stick a light bulb in just about anything.'

— **AMY ADAMS**

Perch! is the brand of ceramicist Amy Adams, who happily combines the production scale of industry with the handmade quality of craft to make refreshing, colourful pieces which are functional, yet sculptural. All of her products are environmentally friendly, using low-impact materials and non-toxic finishes, and she likes her manufacturing to support local workshops and craftspeople. Amy makes ceramic pieces for the garden and the kitchen but has a great collection of lighting, too, with colourful wall sconces, desk lamps and pendant lamps, including her bestselling *Early Bird* pendant light.

Amy has two degrees, having studied art at the University of Iowa and design at the Pratt Institute in Brooklyn. After graduate school she worked with lighting designer David Weeks for five years, during which time she learned how to wire everything from desk lamps to multi-tiered chandeliers. She also did a lot of sourcing for specific lighting parts, so when she

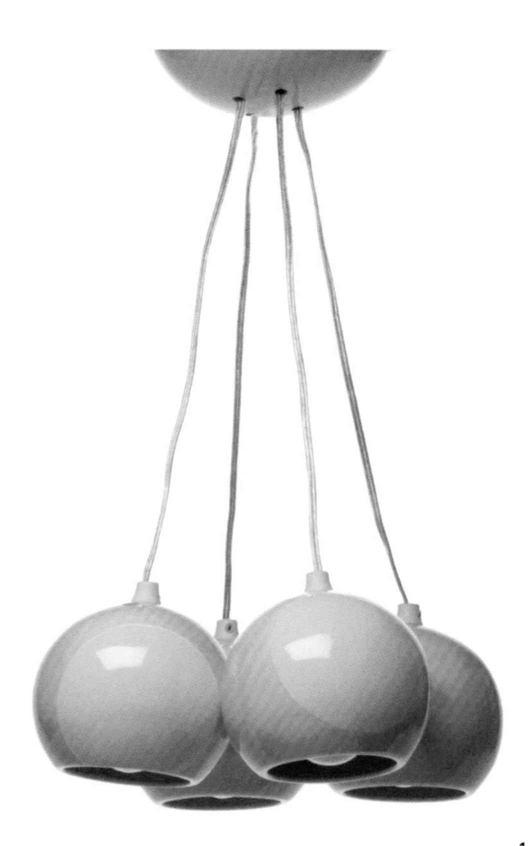

1

1
PERCH!, *ZOOEY MINI CHANDELIER.*
Chandelier made up of four hand-painted ceramic balls held together in a square, 30.5 x 30.5 x 30.5 cm (12 x 12 x 12 in.).
Photo: Robert Bean.

2
PERCH!, *ROUND SCONCES.*
This simple sconce adds some colour to the wall, 15 x 15 x 15 cm (6 x 6 x 6 in.).
Photo: courtesy of the artist.

developed her own lighting range, out of a need to do something 'bigger, better and more complicated', she knew what was involved. 'I think as designers we are good at seeing the potential in materials and taking things out of context, so I was willing to stick a light bulb in just about anything,' she says.

All of Amy's work is made from slip-cast earthenware. She makes a model out of a block of foam, using a lathe if she wants to make it symmetrical. She uses saws and files to rough out the shape and then sands the model down and coats it with something glossy, which makes it easier to clean up later. From this model she makes a plaster mould and casts it in clay. Then she will experiment with how to cut or decorate it. For most of her lights, she may only have one or two moulds, so they are always made to order.

Amy has been living and working in Brooklyn for over thirteen years and takes lots of inspiration from her thriving neighbourhood. She has recently moved to new premises on an historic industrial pier in Red Hook, right across from the Statue of Liberty and surrounded by water and boats. This huge brick warehouse with magnificent arched doorways houses her large ceramic studio and a showroom where she sells one-of-a-kind products and prototypes and a large selection of lighting. 'We run it like a bakery,' says Amy, 'with things coming fresh out of the kiln every day.'

PERCH!, *EARLY BIRD LIGHT.*
The classic *Early Bird* pendant adds a subtle sculptural accent to any room. Light comes out of the top of the wings, the bottom and the tail, 30.5 x 14 x 11 cm (12 x 5½ x 4⅓ in.). *Photo: Claire Abribat.*

SCABETTI, *STAINLESS-STEEL SHOAL, KONOBA BAR, SEYCHELLES.* Stainless-steel installation. Over 7000 stainless steel forms 'swim' across the entire length of the venue on 100 m (328 ft.) of tracking. *Photo: Dusan Kochol.*

Scabetti

UNITED KINGDOM

Scabetti is led by husband and wife duo Dominic and Frances Bromley, based in Leek in Staffordshire. They launched in 1999 and their daughter's childhood word for spaghetti became the inspiration for their business name. Their three children have grown alongside their company and the couple have found a fulfilling balance between work and family life.

Scabetti are most famous for their breath-taking piece *Shoal*, in which hundreds of bone-china fish swirl around

'Daylight brings to life certain colours and enhances the many tonal qualities of the white and the purity of the china.'

— **FRANCES BROMLEY**

a light source. Dominic first launched his career with his *Amoeba* candlestick and a number of other tabletop ceramic pieces. He was confident around ceramics and slip-casting as his father, John Bromley, is a world-renowned figurine sculptor. A few years into his practice Dominic created a large sculptural mobile from many ceramic multiples, which he lit, hoping to attract more people to his trade show stand. The piece, aptly named *Drawn to the Light*, grabbed a lot of attention and marked the beginning of the creation of their sculptural installation pieces.

They were struck by the idea to change the shape of the multiples, and created a fish-shaped mould, taking inspiration for the pattern on its back from the mackerel on their dinner plates. The first piece they made had 284 fish, which multiplied into 1672 when they created their dramatic 1.5 metre (5 ft.) diameter *Shoal*, which they launched at 100% Design in 2007. The piece stopped people in their tracks, and the Bromleys were very pleased to receive orders and requests for installations on the back of this exposure. Jill and Rick Stein fell in love with *Shoal* and it now hangs in their seafood restaurant in Cornwall.

The multiples of fish are cast from bone china, sometimes with a matt finish, sometimes with a shiny glaze, and for their shimmering piece *Goldfish* each is lavishly coated in 24-carat gold. Dominic has a deep understanding of slip-casting and mould-making. Their multiples are handmade by a local ceramic workshop, drawing on the wealth of expertise that still exists in Staffordshire's ceramic industry and supporting their ethos of helping British-made craft.

Light plays a big part in the life of their pieces. 'With *Shoal*, for instance,' says Frances, 'in a darkened environment, when the light shines *on* the fish, you really notice their surface quality. Daylight brings to life certain colours and enhances the many tonal qualities of the white and the purity of the china. But then when you have light shining *through* ... well, it's like when you look in someone's eyes. You look beyond the surface because there's something going on inside.'

1
SCABETTI, *GOLDFISH.*
24-carat gold-plated fine bone china, 85 x 50 x 50 cm (33½ x 19¾ x 19¾ in.). *Photo: Frances Bromley.*

2
SCABETTI, *DRAWN TO THE LIGHT XL.*
Glazed fine bone china. Each form is 18 cm (7 in.) in diameter; full size as sculptural arrangement is 200 cm high, 200 cm in diameter (78¾ x 78¾ in.). *Photo: Frances Bromley.*

3
SCABETTI, *SHOAL1672.*
Fine bone china, 200 x 150 x 150 cm (78¾ x 59 x 59 in.). *Photo: Mark Wood.*

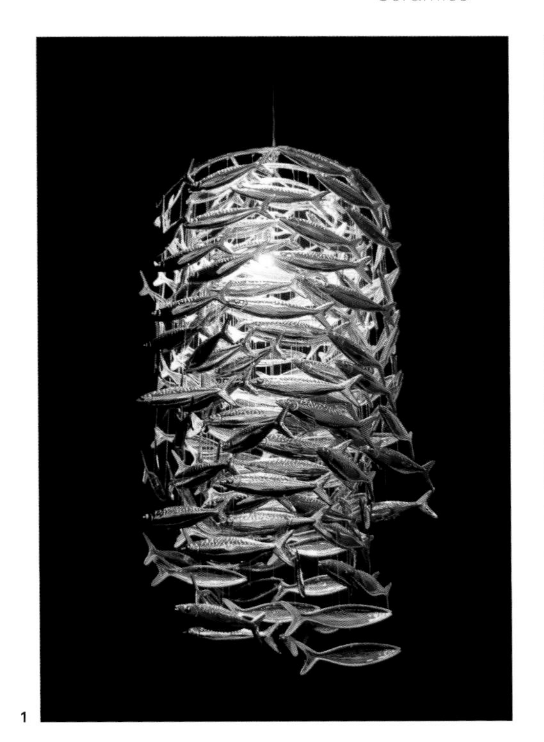
1

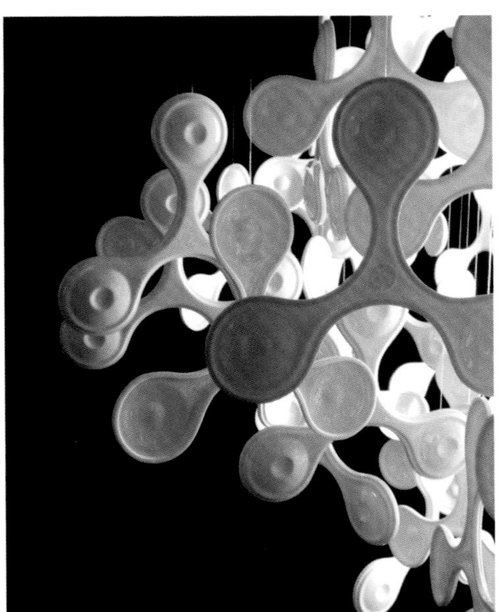
2

3

2 TEXTILES

The six designers in this chapter have all cleverly constructed lighting from a variety of textile-based materials. Shiny ribbons and trimmings provide endless colour combinations for lampshades, silk organza is manipulated to create curious surface textures, organic linen and hemp is printed and constructed into vintage-style shades and printed line drawings, and silk scarves are stitched together to create a mosaic of colour and texture.

With a wealth of techniques up their sleeves, such as embroidering and appliquéing, printing and dyeing, weaving and stitching, it seems that if you put colourful yarn, felt or even VELCRO® into the hands of these designers, these materials will be transformed into something surprising and beautiful, bound to add interest and light to our homes.

ISABEL STANLEY,
HOT RED RIBBON SHADE.
Medium drum in hot red with a medium bottle base and a wenge finish, shade: 15 x 15 x 15 cm (6 x 6 x 6 in.), base height: 22 x 7.5 x 7.5 cm (8¾ x 3 x 3 in.). *Photo: Kev Dutton.*

Rachel O'Neill

IRELAND

'The light creates and exaggerates depths and throws dancing shadows on the walls and ceilings or floors.'

— RACHEL O'NEILL

Irish textile designer Rachel O'Neill experimented with many different kinds of material but found that none of them would hold the shapes that she was trying to make until she discovered VELCRO®. 'It evokes childhood memories of my favourite trainers and schoolbags and when you open it the scratching sound it makes is just so fun.' She found a way to steam the VELCRO® with a special material to create a metallic finish. She also loved how it took to dyes, discovering a way to dye the material in vibrant colours by boiling. Although the colours look muddy during the dyeing process, the results are stunning hot pinks, zesty limes and cool blues.

Rachel uses VELCRO® as her base material and creates large sculptural chandeliers into which she incorporates other materials and objects. She has a collection with feathers and miniature animals and has been known to use Swarovski crystals in some of her work. Rachel has worked on some fabulous commissions, including making chandeliers from 5 km (3 miles) of VELCRO® for Peugeot's concept showrooms in Berlin and Paris. She exhibits widely, and previous shows have included the International Contemporary Furniture Fair (ICFF) in New York, and Maison et Objet in Paris.

The idea of creating lighting came to her accidentally. Running out of space to display her work, O'Neill began to hang it from the ceiling of her studio. One sunny morning the sunlight shone in and hit her pieces, lighting them up and casting lovely shadows around the room. 'I feel light almost gives each piece a personality,' she says. 'The light creates and exaggerates depths and throws dancing shadows on the walls and ceilings or floors.' Although she tries to incorporate different light sources into her work she says that even the simplest bulb can transform a piece.

Rachel loves living in Ireland and says that being surrounded by water has a profound effect on her work, giving it an organic and ever-flowing feel.

1

2

3

1
RACHEL O'NEILL, *NEST LAMP FROM FEATHER COLLECTION.*
Hand-dyed VELCRO® in pink and orange with goose biot feathers, diameter 50 cm (19¾ in.). *Photo: Glenn Norwood.*

2
RACHEL O'NEILL, *WEAVER CHANDELIER FROM FEATHER COLLECTION (DETAIL).*
Hand-dyed VELCRO® in green, hand-dyed goose biot feathers, fibre optics, 65 x 65 x 120 cm (25½ x 25½ x 47¼ in.). *Photo: Glenn Norwood.*

3
RACHEL O'NEILL, *WHISTLE WALL FROM GILDED COLLECTION (DETAIL).*
Silver-foiled VELCRO®, 120 x 120 x 5 cm (47¼ x 47¼ in.). *Photo: Glenn Norwood.*

Ai Kawauchi

JAPAN

'When I speak to friends or people around me, or when I receive letters from my close friends, that is when I become filled with inspiration'.

— AI KAWAUCHI

Japanese artist Ai Kawauchi makes illuminated textile-art pieces. Her lighting collection *White and Silk* is made with an intricate and unique technique using silk organza from the Kiryū region of Japan, as well as traditional Japanese washi paper. The pieces vary in shape and size and hang like white, fluffy clouds.

The base of each light is a papier mâché form made from many layers of washi paper. This paper is much stronger than ordinary paper, so it makes a good base on which to lay her fabric. The bobbles are made by tying silk organza around many small glass beads or balls and leaving it to soak in a carefully calculated solution of acids. After some time, the organza is removed from the solution, washed thoroughly and left to dry completely. The beads are then removed one by one, leaving their shape behind in the organza. This newly structured 'bobbly' fabric is then attached to the washi base.

1

Whilst Ai was studying textiles at Joshibi University of Art and Design in Tokyo, she was introduced to many new materials and practices in a very stimulating environment. She began investigating simple tie-dye effects and this evolved into the technique she uses to create her shapes and forms. As well as making her lights, she works on a much smaller scale, creating delicate jewellery pieces in the same way.

Ai lives in the south of Japan in the Saga prefecture. Her home is in the quiet countryside and near the beach. 'It is very

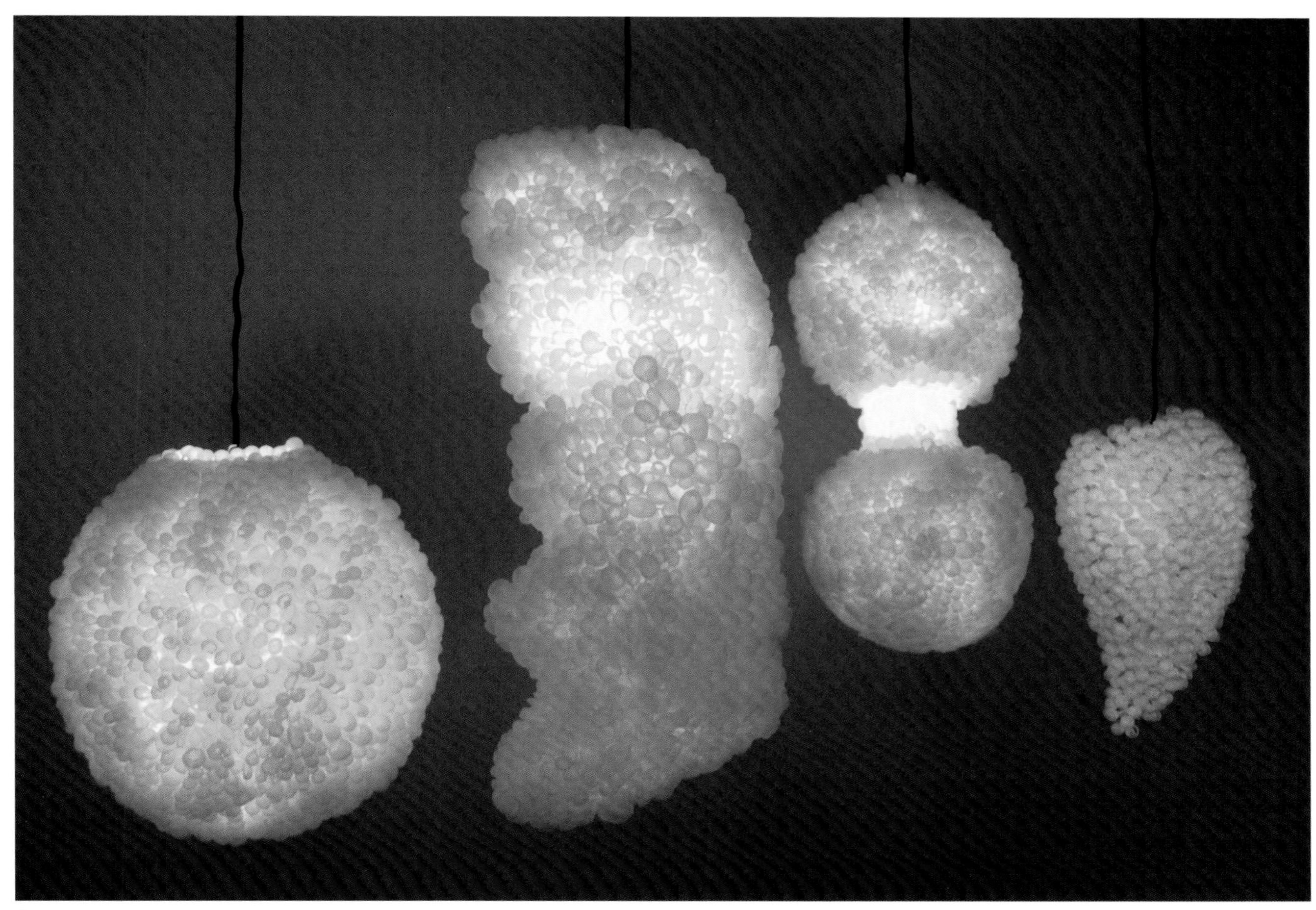

2

1
AI KAWAUCHI, *KYU (DETAIL).*
A light piece from the *White & Silk* collection. *Photo: courtesy of the artist.*

2
AI KAWAUCHI, *KYU, TSUKURU, INORU AND NEKKO.*
Light pieces from the *White & Silk* collection, diameter from left to right: 40 cm (15¾ in.), 17 cm (6¾ in.), 25 cm (10 in.), 16 cm (6⅓ in.). *Photo: courtesy of the artist.*

tranquil and peaceful with good food and beautiful natural scenery. My creative mind is stimulated by all these beautiful colours and organic shapes, which is then reflected in my creative output,' she says. Ai lived in London for a few years, which she loved, introducing her work at Origin Craft Fair and meeting many artists and craft fans.

For Ai, interactions with people are the biggest force for her creativity. She has friends in different fields of art and design, like architecture and photography, and finds that this helps her to see things from a different perspective, motivating her and helping her work to evolve. She says, 'When I speak to friends or people around me, or when I receive letters from my close friends, that is when I become filled with inspiration.'

Ana Kraš

SERBIA

'They are like jewellery for the house, and the way they shine changes the space more than anything else.'

— **ANA KRAŠ**

Ana Kraš studied interior architecture and furniture design at the University of Applied Arts in Belgrade, where she grew up. At the time, she says, her university and in fact her whole country were in disarray. There were not really any workshops and not a single computer, which angered her, but looking back she can see the good in it: 'It makes you try harder to make something out of nothing.'

She can't remember what inspired her to make her *Bonbon* lamps except that one day the idea was there in her mind and the very next day she had her first metal frame constructed and tried wrapping strands of wool around it to see if it would work.

Inspired by her prototype she approached a knitwear company who donated lots of wool left over from old collections. 'I remember at first I was scared that no one would accept my colours,' she says. 'I wanted to add something happy and attractive, but they are a bit like my grandmother's closet!'

She makes her work in very small editions and every lamp is totally different. The frames vary in shape and she loves that there are so many possibilities with them. Each lamp takes a long time to make: first she takes a drawing of the frame to the metalworker and after this is made it goes to the powder-coaters. She then begins her work building on the frame. Colourful wool is painstakingly wrapped around the frame, a process that can take up to 25 hours depending on its size. Her back and her hands hurt afterwards – 'and my head,' she says, 'it asks for concentration.' Her *Bonbons* are designed to be suspended from the ceiling but she also makes an elegant floor-lamp version called *The Hive*, which is a simple construction made from wood and wingnuts.

Her lamps look so joyful hung together, like one big family, all similar but varying in shape and colour. 'Lamps are very different from other furniture,' says Ana. 'They are like jewellery for the house, and the way they shine changes the space more than anything else.'

1

2

3

1
ANA KRAŠ, *BONBON LAMP.*
Cream and blue wool knitted manually over a steel frame, 35 x 30 x 30 cm (13¾ x 12 x 12 in.). *Photo: Ana Kraš*

3
ANA KRAŠ, *BONBON LAMPS AND LAMPSHADE FRAMES.*
A group of *Bonbon* lamps and their frames, dimensions variable. *Photo: Ana Kraš.*

2
ANA KRAŠ, *HIVE LAMP.*
Floor lamp with an oak body and a *Bonbon* lampshade, 160 x 73 x 30 cm (63 x 28¾ x 12 in.). *Photo: Ana Kraš.*

Maartje van den Noort

THE NETHERLANDS

'The idea of having light shining through the fabrics and expressing my drawings and the textures makes me happy.'

— **MAARTJE VAN DEN NOORT**

Dutch artist Maartje van den Noort loves to draw. For years she has kept sketchbooks full of expressive line drawings of birds; finches, blue tits and woodpeckers, often larger than life, can be found perched on top of tiny buildings, telegraph wires, cars and lampposts. These beautiful drawings have become the basis of everything that she produces.

Maartje studied graphic design and fine arts in Rotterdam. Then in 2006 the owners of Restored, a shop in Amsterdam selling handmade design, were looking at ways to light their first retail space, and asked her to decorate some paper lanterns with her drawings. She discovered that the best way to do this was by using fabrics with her drawings on them and thus the idea for her *Lappion* lamps was born. These spherical textile structures are made from different panels of fabrics including silkscreen prints of her own drawings. Her prints are nestled amongst different coloured and textured panels of fabrics. No two lampshades are ever the same.

Maartje finds new and second-hand fabrics in thrift stores or from the Dappermarkt close to her home in Amsterdam. She sends fabric to be silk-screen printed with her drawings, sometimes just with black ink but occasionally with gold or white. Once she has the printed fabrics back she starts picking colours, prints and textures to complement each other and then sews them together piece by piece. In the end she finishes the top and the bottom with a tunnel on both sides through which to feed elastic. She then 'folds' the work around a paper globe lantern, draws the elastic tight and finishes the last seam.

'The idea of having light shining through the fabrics and expressing my drawings and the textures makes me happy,' says Maartje. 'When the light is turned on, but even when it is not, the Lappion gives a warming welcome to a room.'

AT WOONBEURS 2010, AMSTERDAM.
Maartje at work during the home and interior fair in Amsterdam, Autumn 2010.
Photo: Marijke Hukema.

1

2

1
MAARTJE VAN DEN NOORT, *SMALL LAPPION WITH DRAWINGS SILK-SCREEN PRINTED ON THE FABRIC.*
Diameter 45 cm (17¾ in.).
Photo: Hannah Nunn.

2
MAARTJE VAN DEN NOORT, *LAPPION (DETAIL).*
Photo: Hannah Nunn.

Maartje lives in the eastern part of Amsterdam and loves it for being 'vibrant but not hectic', with a mixture of cultures and a laidback atmosphere. She cycles to her studio, located in an old sailor's home with a lovely high ceiling and grand stairs. Travelling and having free time leaves her mind open to new input, but daily life is her biggest inspiration, from the people she meets every day to the birds in her backyard.

Maxine Sutton

UNITED KINGDOM

Since graduating from the MA course in Constructed Textiles at the Royal College of Art in 2005, Maxine Sutton has gone on to develop her collection of hand-printed and embroidered wall pieces, textile pictures and, more recently, functional 3D pieces in the form of lampshades.

Maxine uses natural fabrics and particularly loves to work on linens, hemp and organic cotton. She uses both new and recycled lampshade frames and re-covers them with her own fabrics. 'People do seem to love the combination of a contemporary fabric on a traditional-shaped shade,' she says.

Each shade develops as a one-off piece. Maxine creates layers of colour and form and adds embroidered details until she feels the composition is balanced and interesting. The shades are made from bias-cut fabric pieces. Colour can be a starting point and she usually spends a considerable amount of time mixing and stirring up a new palette of colours to work with. She has hand-drawn patterns ready-prepared on screens and then, working from her sketchbooks and drawings, she hand-cuts a variety of paper stencils and starts printing her fabric.

The embroidery usually comes as a final embellishment, like an accent. After screen-printing, the pieces are cured and given to a skilled local shade-maker to be sewn, stretched and stitched in place.

MAXINE SUTTON,
THREE HANGING SHADES.
Diameters range between 30 and 75 cm (12 and 29½ in.), height between 20 and 30 cm (8 and 12 in.). *Photo: courtesy of the artist.*

1

Maxine's studio is above a small shop called Blackbird that she runs in Margate Old Town, which sells contemporary handmade artwork, interior pieces and gifts while offering studio spaces and courses in hand-printing and stitching upstairs. This lovely, characterful building provides much inspiration, being near the sea and the beach and having beautiful views of the sky and sunsets at the end of the street.

Maxine always finds it exciting to see the flat pieces of work she has laboured over arrive back at her shop as beautifully-made 3D objects. Sitting them on a lamp base and lighting them up is yet another cause for excitement. 'It's really interesting to see how different colours and textures react with the light inside,' she says, 'but mainly it's just so satisfying to see something you've conceived and hand-worked coming alive through its function and use. When a customer falls in love with a piece you've made, enough to want to take it home with them, that's the ultimate reward and satisfaction.'

1
MAXINE SUTTON, *SHADE CLUSTER.*
Screen-printed, embroidered pendant lightshades, 40 x 26 x 26 cm (15¾ x 10¼ x 10¼ in.). *Photo: courtesy of the artist.*

2

3

4

2

MAXINE SUTTON, *SCREEN-PRINTED AND EMBROIDERED LIGHTSHADE (DETAIL).*

Photo: courtesy of the artist.

3

MAXINE SUTTON, *ALEXIA SHADE.*

Screen-printed and embroidered hand-tailored lightshade, 74 x 30 x 30 cm (29 x 12 x 12 in.). *Photo: courtesy of the artist.*

4

MAXINE SUTTON, *ALEXIA SHADE (DETAIL).*

Screen-printed and embroidered natural linen shade. *Photo: courtesy of the artist.*

Isabel Stanley

UNITED KINGDOM

'The intense colours of the ribbon sing when the lamp is switched on.'

— **ISABEL STANLEY**

Isabel Stanley is well-known for her stripy ribbon lampshades in luscious colours. The Conran Shop has been selling Isabel's work since 1997, and the first colourway she designed for them is still a bestseller even to this day. Her work has been sold worldwide, adorning many interior spaces, including the famous café Pret A Manger.

Following a BA in Textiles and Embroidery at Goldsmiths College in London, Isabel worked as an embroiderer for years, creating samples for an agent and lecturing in embroidery at the London College of Fashion. She wrote projects for magazines and authored several books on embroidery and home accessories. The research carried out whilst she wrote her most recent book on lampshades revealed that many at the time were bland, old-fashioned and disappointing. She wanted to create something vibrant and colourful, so she used bands of velvet ribbon that she had found on her travels in Guatemala, and made a lampshade as a project for the book. Her readers loved it and she soon realised she had to develop it into a product.

Her shades come in many drum sizes and are made from satin, velvet, petersham and haberdashery ribbon overlapped in simple stripes on to lampshade PVC. Her converted loft studio at home in East Dulwich, London, is 'a riot of colour', she says, 'with Perspex boxes crammed full of ribbons and fabric, postcards and samples haphazardly pinned to the walls.' Making the shades by hand allows for an infinite number of colour combinations. Isabel demonstrates her artistic eye in collections such as *Mineral Ice*, *Cobalt & Daffodil* and *Magenta Moss*. Colour combinations can be custom-made to suit a client's own vision of the perfect colour mix.

Her shades have a luxurious feel and the craftsmanship is impeccable. 'The intense colours of the ribbon sing when the lamp is switched on,' says Isabel. They have a liveliness that grabs your attention and, on or off, they brighten up any room.

2

1

1
ISABEL STANLEY, *EXTRA WIDE RIBBON DRUM.*
Extra-wide drum in old gold and extra-large fifties base with a wenge finish, 18 x 25 x 25 cm (7 x 9¾ x 9¾ in.). *Photo: Kev Dutton.*

2
ISABEL STANLEY, *RIBBON SHADE IN GREEN, SKY AND YELLOW.*
Wide cylinder in striped ribbon collection in bottle green/sky/yellow on an extra-large fifties base, shade: 23 x 23 x 23 cm (9 x 9 x 9 in.), base: 27 x 10 x 10 cm (10½ x 4 x 4 in.). *Photo: Kev Dutton.*

3 PAPER

Folding, creasing, cutting, gluing, bonding, shaping, sculpting: the artists in this chapter have a passion for paper and have found many interesting ways of using it to create lights, offering a modern take on some very traditional art forms.

Paper cutting, an ancient tradition in many cultures across the world, lends itself well to light, with cut shapes creating strong silhouettes in front of a window or a light source. This is indeed what inspired me to make my own lamps. The ancient Japanese art of origami and paper folding has been brought to light here too, with three-dimensional geometric forms being lit from within to highlight every crease and fold. Papier mâché, well known for its strength, is used to create large sculptural light forms and colourful glowing lanterns and chandeliers.

Drawing from the wealth of beautiful papers available, or creating their own from scratch using plant and vegetable fibres, these artists have realised that the qualities of paper are greatly enriched by interaction with light. Each of them has found a very different way of demonstrating this in their work but the same particular feeling of warmth is emitted from every paper creation.

HANNAH NUNN, *SEED POD TABLE LAMP*.
A one-off table lamp with a paper-cut seed pod design, 30 x 13 x 13 cm (12 x 5 x 5 in.).
Photo: Andrew Sanderson.

Hannah Nunn

UNITED KINGDOM

'I love cutting through the paper with my scalpel because it's like drawing with light.'

— HANNAH NUNN

HANNAH NUNN, *DANDELION CLOCKS LAMP.*
A table lamp with a laser-cut and engraved dandelion clocks design, 30 x 13 x 13 cm (12 x 5 x 5 in.).
Photo: Andrew Sanderson.

I make paper-cut lamps inspired by my love of the botanical world. My lamps seem to speak to people who love nature as I do, enjoying the alliums, harebells, snowdrops or dandelion seeds blowing in the wind.

I studied crafts in Carmarthen, and lived in Laugharne, a beautiful, sleepy town on the Welsh coast. I had my two children soon after leaving college and in my snatches of free time I would go out with my sketchbook to make detailed flower drawings (which would later become the inspiration for my lamp designs) and dream of starting a creative business.

In 1999 we settled in Hebden Bridge, a vibrant arty town in Yorkshire, surrounded by stunning woodland and countryside. I rented a small space in a shared studio and began by making a range of paper-cut greetings cards which sold really well across the country. I was forever holding the cards up to the light to enjoy their silhouettes so, when my friend suggested I make lamps, I was instantly inspired! With Arts Council funding and a lot of experimentation I created my first collection of paper-cut lighting. I took it to the British Craft Trade Fair and, after a successful show, my career in craft lighting began.

I work with 300gsm parchment as it has a lovely, warm glow when lit and looks clean and simple when not. I make my designs by cutting, layering and laser-engraving the paper to create varying degrees of light and shadow. I design on a light box with a translucent cutting mat and I love cutting through the paper with my scalpel because it's like drawing with light; I can immediately see what the design will look like when it is lit. Then I laminate the paper, not only for strength and durability but to create a translucent layer that appears bright and white when lit. The light is the final ingredient, enhancing every crisply cut line and twinkling through the tiny pinpricks.

My range has grown to include table lamps, wall pieces, floor lamps and intricate fairy lights, and as well as having a large selection of designs for people to

1

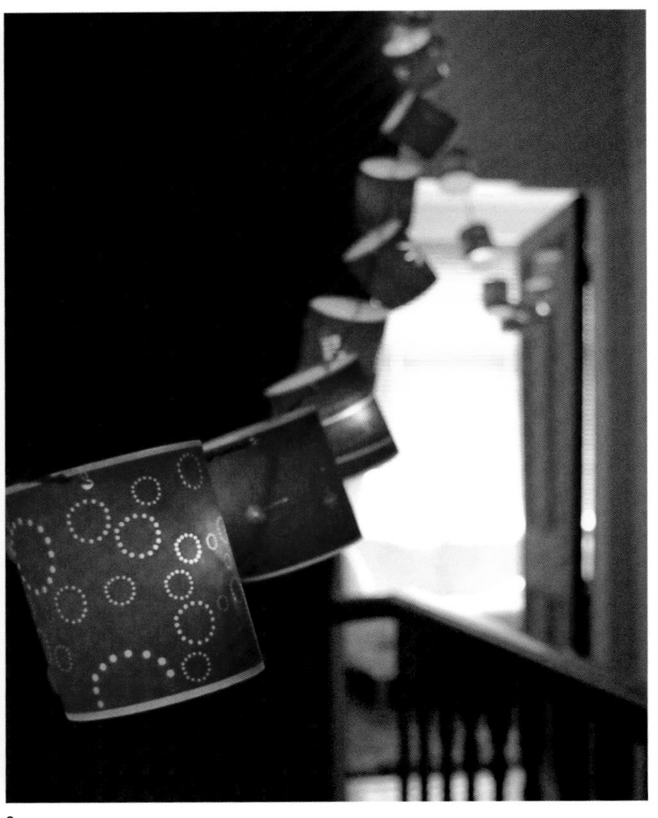
2

1
HANNAH NUNN, *SMALL ALLIUM LAMP.*
A table lamp with a laser-cut allium design, 30 x 13 x 13 cm (12 x 5 x 5 in.). *Photo: Andrew Sanderson.*

2
HANNAH NUNN, *FAIRY LIGHTS.*
A string of glowing paper-cut lanterns. Fairy light string 500 cm (16 ft. 5 in.) long, each lantern 7 cm (2¾ in.) high. *Photo: Hannah Nunn.*

choose from, I also make one-off art pieces and bespoke, personalised lamps.

Creating my own range sparked a passion for other people's handmade lighting and in 2005 I opened my shop Radiance so that I could bring it all together in one glowing space. I have my workshop at the back of the shop and I enjoy the balance between creating and sourcing lovely work for the shop. I love hearing the stories of how the work came about, which I guess is what led me to write this book.

I have a lot to thank my friend for. Her idea that I should make lamps has blossomed into a career and found me my niche in the craft-lighting world.

Andrew Ooi

CANADA

'Every day, and everything, inspires.'

— ANDREW OOI

Andrew Ooi is a Toronto-based free-folding artist. He was first introduced to origami in his early twenties by a friend who showed him how to make a paper crane. At the time he had a long commute to university and he enjoyed working his way through origami fundamentals with the free newspaper. The skills he learned during these many long hours of travelling became the foundation for the more advanced paper folding he has perfected today. He creates incredible geometric forms entirely held together by interlocking individual units. No glue, tape or any kind of adhesive is ever used.

One day, he saw one of his geometric pieces close to a pendant lamp. 'The

ANDREW OOI, *MOKUME WALNUT LIGHT*.
Mokume paper with a walnut base, 30.5 x 30.5 x 35.5 cm (12 x 12 x 14 in.).
Photo: Yumiko Miyamoto.

1

2

1
ANDREW OOI, *SONOBE LIGHT (DETAIL).*
Made from folded Fabriano Tiziano paper with silk-screened design and a bookbinding clasp. *Photo: Yumiko Miyamoto.*

2
ANDREW OOI, *SONOBE LIGHT.*
Made from folded Fabriano Tiziano paper with silk-screened design and a bookbinding clasp, diameter 38 cm (15 in.). *Photo: Yumiko Miyamoto.*

way the piece had captured the light, displaying subtleties in shade and brilliance in pattern, was so striking it was impossible to ignore,' says Andrew. He reassembled the adjoining individual units to accommodate a light fitting and felt a whole new appreciation for the artwork. Now the process and the patterning of the folding could be shown as an intrinsic part of the work itself.

Every crease Andrew makes in the paper is formed with intent and care, and he hopes that lighting his pieces helps to illuminate those thoughts and feelings. The type of paper determines the variation in shadows cast, patterns lit up and overall warmth, so the paper is chosen with the right characteristic in mind for the piece he wants to create. He has discovered that watercolour papers such as Fabriano Tiziano retain their shape really well and can withstand excessive folding. Handmade Japanese papers, such as Gampi Udaban, have the right kind of

3

malleability and can happily accept and smooth away creases while folding. 'I am an intuitive folder,' says Andrew. 'My folding is based on experimenting with and expanding upon my familiarity with the behaviour of standard origami folds.' This kind of improvisation, or 'free folding', allows Andrew to problem-solve as he goes along, discovering which way to go next while he works. Although he uses some preliminary sketches and concepts, he mostly relies on the paper to influence the finished form.

His biggest source of inspiration is simply being open to seeing things. 'Every day, and everything, inspires. It could be the rows and columns of windows on tall, glass office buildings, or the subtle striations and arrangement of barbs on a bird feather.' He obviously notices pattern, order and how things relate to one another. We can see clearly how this inspiration and acute observation translates into artworks made with fine mastery and skill.

3
ANDREW OOI, *MOKUME WALNUT LIGHT.*
Mokume paper with a walnut base,
18 x 18 x 38 cm (7 x 7 x 15 in.).
Photo: Yumiko Miyamoto.

Louise Traill

UNITED KINGDOM

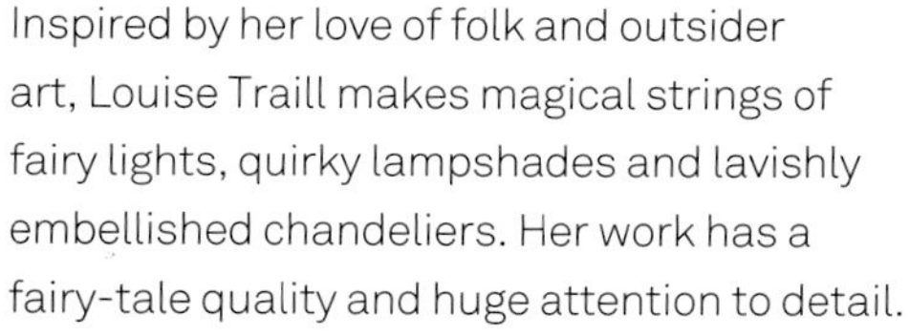

Inspired by her love of folk and outsider art, Louise Traill makes magical strings of fairy lights, quirky lampshades and lavishly embellished chandeliers. Her work has a fairy-tale quality and huge attention to detail.

1

Originally from Scarborough, Louise studied at the Chelsea School of Art and after graduating in 1992 she travelled to Israel and Egypt. She came home, attained a PGCE teaching certificate, and went to Botswana to teach. Inspired by the local craft there but with nowhere to buy a lamp for her lodgings, she decided to make one herself from wire and paper. 'It was a bit wonky,' says Louise, but she found it charming and it inspired her to explore the idea further.

On her return to the UK she set about finding some stockists for her lamps and rented retail space at Gabriel's Wharf in London. Things grew from there until her lights could be found in galleries up and down the country including the prestigious lighting department at Liberty of London. She moved to a cottage near Malton in North Yorkshire and opened a glowing little shop called Halo in the centre of York, where she worked for six years.

All her pieces begin with a framework constructed from wire, which she covers with paper chosen for its colour, texture, pattern and translucent qualities. Louise has a vast collection of handmade and unusual papers as well as a colourful assortment of beads, sequins, trimmings, tassels and buttons, which she uses to adorn her pieces. She has been making her *Heirloom Lights* for around 12 years now. Although they have developed subtly over the years, their essentially timeless quality has endured through many changes in fashion and trends.

Over the years she has thought about getting a dedicated studio space but has come to realise that she's happier creating work in her own home, from her kitchen table, which enables her to be around for her young son. With her lights in high demand, people have tried to encourage her to get them made abroad to speed up

2

3

1, 2
LOUISE TRAILL, *HEIRLOOM LIGHTS.*
A handmade paper lantern, each lantern 14 x 8 x 8 cm (5½ x 3 x 3 in.).
Photo: Hannah Nunn.

3
LOUISE TRAILL, *THREE-TIER CHANDELIER (DETAIL).*
Three-tier paper chandelier, 61 x 40 x 40 cm (24 x 15¾ x 15¾ in.).
Photo: Hannah Nunn.

production, but Louise thinks this misses the point, that each should be hand-crafted. At busy times she prefers hiring friendly help and having everyone gather in her cottage garden for afternoons of lantern making and tea drinking. It's not particularly about speed, but rather putting care and concentration into each and every light. This love for her work and close attention to craftsmanship really come through when her lights are illuminated.

Céline Wright

FRANCE

1

'Nature is the heart of my inspiration.'

— **CÉLINE WRIGHT**

Parisian designer/maker Céline Wright has always been interested in lights, even during her first jobs in the fashion industry, as she always saw light as the best medium to reveal materials. The owner of Cour intérieur, an art gallery located on boulevard Beaumarchais in Paris, asked her to create objects based on the theme of the Arabian Nights. On completing the project and seeing the pieces she had created with recycled paper, she was inspired to develop her own lighting range.

It is easy to understand that the beautiful sculptural paper lights she now creates have been inspired by the natural world; they look like a part of nature themselves. Their soft organic shapes follow natural forms, like those of cocoons, clouds, eggs and planets, and they take names such as *Nuage* (cloud), *Kaze* (wind in Japanese) and *Petite Lune* (little moon). They have a Zen-like simplicity about them and a real energy you can sense from the work and craftsmanship that has gone into creating each one.

She uses shōji paper (used to make traditional Japanese screens) as she found that it produced a smooth glow, was very strong, very light and also fire-safe. She makes a resin mould, then pastes on the paper strip by strip, as if making a skin. Once dry, the paper is taken off the mould, creating her shape. The larger lamps, like *Cirrus*, have a metal structure inside which holds the shape and allows it to be fixed to the ceiling.

Céline works in the former Usines Chapal in Montreuil in the suburbs of Paris, alongside her team of six people. They work as a family, with a dynamic team spirit, each one bringing their own know-how. 'It is very important that my creations are handmade,' says Céline, 'as it gives a human relationship aspect. As my producing process respects ecology and is non-polluting, it also satisfies our clients in their demand for a personalised product. Therefore my process is the opposite of mass consumption and industrial process.'

2

Céline has worked with a large number of architects and interior designers and loves to see her lighting in the many beautiful and prestigious venues that she has designed for, including the lobby of ski company Rossignol's headquarters. Seeing her lighting within nature itself also brings her happiness. 'Nature is the heart of my inspiration,' she says. 'Silent, quiet and lonely landscapes are my favourite source of inspiration. Being aware of rays of light, sounds in the trees and even clouds, constitute ideas for creating.'

1
CÉLINE WRIGHT, *KAZE.*
A lightweight paper architecture perched high on a steel mast. Made from Japanese paper and black cast steel, 176 x 100 x 60 cm (69¼ x 39¼ x 23½ in.). *Photo: Virginie Perocheau.*

2
CÉLINE WRIGHT, *POINT DE SUSPENSION.*
Japanese paper with a white marble pebble, 50 x 40 x 250 cm (19¾ x 15¾ x 98½ in.). *Photo: Virginie Perocheau.*

HiiH Lights

UNITED STATES

'There is a magic to our collaboration.'

— **LÂM QUÁNG AND KESTREL GATES**

HiiH Lights, pronounced 'Hi Hi', is the creation of husband-and-wife team Lâm Quáng and Kestrel Gates, who are based in Portland, Oregon. Their tagline sums up just what their work is about: 'The function of light, the craft of paper and the art of sculpture.' Their warm and functional pieces can be found in residential and commercial settings across the US.

Lâm's experiments with papermaking began in the 1990s. He blended everything he could find – sugar cane, mulberry bark, hemp, even potatoes! Holding his papers up to a light source and seeing the fibres physically bonding and weaving together inspired him to make lamps and lanterns.

After playing with this idea in his studio, he plucked up the courage to introduce his works to the public. In 1998 Alberta Street in Portland, now a thriving arts district, was beginning its resurgence after a long dormant period. He found a storefront studio there and opened HiiH Gallery, where he could continue to develop his work and sell it at the same time.

In 2004 he met Kestrel and they began to collaborate closely on all their pieces, inspiring each other to keep creating and exploring. They now work together from their large studio, with plate-glass walls that overlook their garden, so they can keep creating and exploring at home and be near their two young children.

Making a lamp is an involved process. They first build a unique armature from wire or bamboo, which will

1

2

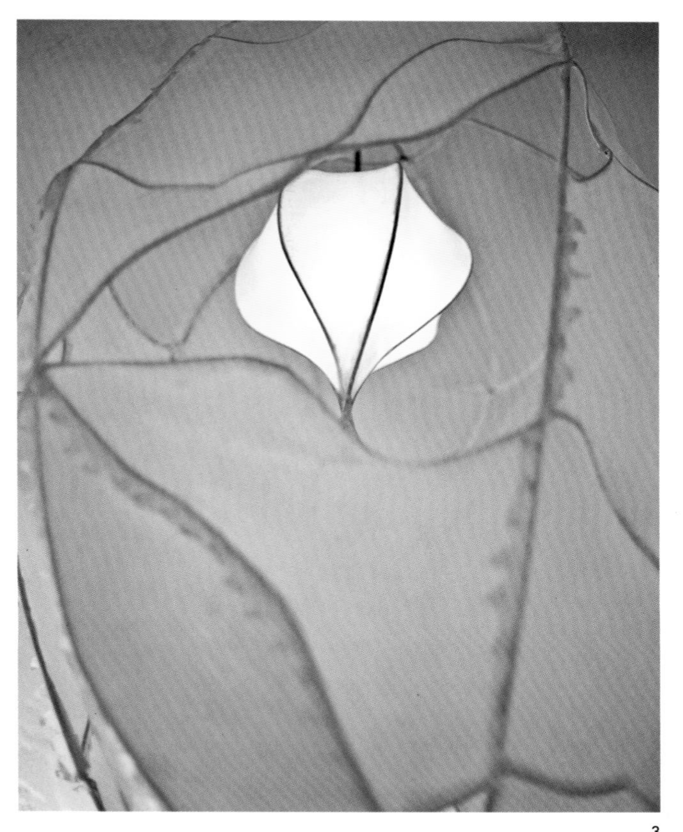

3

1
HIIH LIGHTS, *PURPLE LOTUS.*
Oil lantern at the Portland Chinese Garden, 45.5 x 30.5 x 30.5 cm (18 x 12 x 12 in.). *Photo: Kestrel Gates.*

2
HIIH LIGHTS, *CHRYSANTHEMUM.*
Artist-made paper sconce, 38 x 38 x 38 cm (15 x 15 x 15 in.). *Photo: Leah Verwey.*

3
HIIH LIGHTS, *LIFE INSIDE CACOON.*
Artist-made paper pendant, 91.5 x 61 x 61 cm (36 x 24 x 24 in.). *Photo: Leah Verwey.*

be covered with paper one sheet at a time. The sheets of paper are made using a mould and deckle: cotton and abaca pulp is passed through the mould, a fine mesh held in a wooden frame, and when the excess water drains away, the resulting layer of pulp is shaped with the deckle, a second frame that fits inside the mould. They use an eight-tonne press to bind the fibres and then apply the damp sheets to the armature, folding over the edges with a damp brush so the paper sticks to itself. Once dried, watercolour paint is applied and followed by resin or beeswax (supplied by a beekeeping neighbour), which forms a protective layer and gives a translucent glow. The last step is fitting the electrical components. 'These steps are all interspersed with tea drinking, cooking, parenting and running errands,' says Lâm. 'What we enjoy most is the creative dialogue that happens throughout the entire process – there is a magic to our collaboration.'

4 PRINT

The seven designers featured in this chapter come from a variety of disciplines, including photography, illustration, surface pattern design, constructed textiles and craft. The thing that links them together is the medium of print. Whether silkscreen printing, monoprinting, digital printing or even using a 3D printer, they all turned to print as a way to get the images they had created on to a new surface – or in the case of 3D printing, to create a new surface altogether.

The simple cylindrical drum lampshade makes the perfect canvas for these prints, allowing them to take centre stage in a room. It gives the artwork an added domestic function, making it more accessible.

Flip the light switch and the print is transformed. Besides the print, other aspects of the work are revealed too, perhaps highlighting the texture of a base cloth or illuminating tiny embroidered pinpricks. We are able, literally, to see the print in a brand new light.

LUSH DESIGNS, *MONKEY SHADE IN BROWN AND GREY.*
29 x 28 x 28 cm (11½ x 11 x 11 in.).
Photo: Jefferson Smith.

Lush Designs

UNITED KINGDOM

Design duo Marie Rodgers and Maria Livings met at art school when they were studying painting and printmaking at Maidstone. After college, they got involved in community arts, making props and outlandish homemade costumes for theatre productions. The outsized sculptural jewellery they created became a successful business called Lushlobes, which in 1994 morphed into Lush Designs when they started moving into homeware.

Their quirky collection of lampshades delight and surprise, and people are entertained by the unusual collection of characters: cheeky monkeys swinging through fantastical forests, a mother fox nestling her cubs amongst the foxgloves, a majestic stag in a moorland landscape, even a skeletal lady being nibbled by fishes in the River Thames! It is clear that the peculiar and the humorous drive their creativity, and this endless stream of ideas is delivered with great charm.

Marie has a love for rhythm and pattern and Maria likes narrative ideas, so these interests combine to form the unique Lush Designs style. They began by screen-printing everything themselves, but after a while they found a screen-printer for all their products, which freed them up to create new designs and colours, run their thriving wholesale business and online store, and look after their beautiful shop in Greenwich. Maria finds the shop a great place to 'draw and dream up ideas', and Marie works in their studio at Cockpit Arts, making lampshades and taking care of the wholesale side of the business.

They both love lampshades, 'partly because you can make a picture that goes round and meets itself coming,' says Maria, 'and also because of what light does to colour, opacity and translucency.' Their shades are made in all sizes from small to huge, and come in a range of refreshing colours.

1

2

3

1

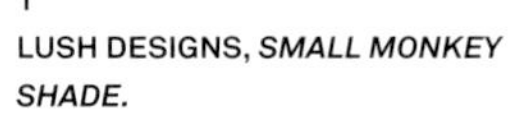

LUSH DESIGNS, *SMALL MONKEY SHADE.*
Lampshade with a monkey print,
20 x 17 x 17 cm (8 x 6¾ x 6¾ in.).
Photo: Hannah Nunn.

2
LUSH DESIGNS, *WILD WEST HORSE LAMPSHADE.*
A Wild West horse amidst cacti,
25 x 24 x 24 cm (9¾ x 9½ x 9½ in.).
Photo: Hannah Nunn.

3
LUSH DESIGNS, *FOX LAMPSHADE.*
Lampshade with a red fox print,
26 x 35 x 35 cm (10¼ 13¾ x 13¾ in.).
Photo: Hannah Nunn.

1

HELEN MINNS, *HARE IN GRASS.*
Hand-printed linen shades, 42 x 34 cm (16½ x 13½ in). *Photo: Helen Minns.*

Helen Minns

UNITED KINGDOM

Helen Minns studied textile design at Central St Martins in London, specialising in printmaking. Soon after college she found herself running a company with a friend, selling printed bags and accessories. This became successful very quickly, but Helen found that she wasn't all that passionate about fashion and left the company to start her family. Two children later and Helen was yearning to create again. She started embroidering at home, took a refresher course in printmaking, joined various evening classes in upholstery and etching and, most importantly, remembered just how much she loved to print. Etching was a great way of experimenting with mark-making on a small scale and seemed the perfect place to start with her textile design.

2

3

Helen's work is very illustrative, and she liked the idea of having a picture on a lampshade, like a canvas with a very practical use. She printed up fabrics and found that linen worked well with her images and colours, as well as being lovely when illuminated. She did lots of research into lampshade manufacturers to find someone to make them up for her so that she could concentrate on printing alone, as that was what she really enjoyed. At first she screen-printed everything in her studio at Cockpit Arts but nowadays, as well as keeping on her studio, she has joined a printmakers' cooperative, which allows her lots of space and access to great facilities.

Helen has vast inspirations. Colour, fabrics, pattern and abstract art all play their part in her work, but it is a love of British wildlife that inspired her current collection, an elegant hare poised in long grass becoming her signature design. 'I think we're just always fascinated by animals and birds, especially wild animals, because they seem to live in this other world,' says Helen. 'We seem to see ourselves as something separate, but the need to be connected is still there.'

2
HELEN MINNS, *BLUE HARE IN GRASS.*
Hand-printed linen shades, 20 x 16 cm (8 x 6¼ in.). *Photo: Hannah Nunn.*

3
HELEN MINNS, *GOLD BIRD LAMPSHADE.*
Hand-printed linen lightshade, 26 x 36 x 36 cm (10¼ x 14 x 14 in.). *Photo: Andrew Porter.*

House of Chintz

UNITED KINGDOM

'It's contrast that I love the best, and light really brings that out.'

— KATE BOYCE

Before Kate Boyce launched her brand House of Chintz, she worked as an interior textile designer for many years, creating floral fabrics and wallpapers. With a desire to develop her own body of work, rather than work to a brief, she started to paint, drawing heavily on a deep feeling for her local landscape in West Yorkshire and developing her distinctive style and technique. After a while she felt the need to combine the two disciplines and wanted to bring pattern into her paintings. Whilst playing with imagery on her computer one day, she found that she had arrived not at an idea for a painting, but for a lampshade.

This arrival was the beginning of an absorbing project taking, as she puts it, 'a light-hearted look at the surroundings I grew up in – the suburban landscape of middle England.' The designs are a combination of her own photographic imagery of the streets where she grew up in Lichfield and digital scans of floral fabric from the 70s and 80s, taking her back to her roots designing 'chintzy' floral patterns. She has always found it engaging to observe how suburban houses are often filled with stylised versions of nature in the form of co-ordinating fabrics and furnishings, which illustrates to her that even in the concrete jungle of housing estates, nature still have an important role to play. Kate has superimposed these familiar fabric patterns on to her photos of the external environment, and brought nature back indoors in the form of lampshades, which create a nostalgic atmosphere by referencing an entire era of British life, the 60s and 70s.

Kate loves the fusion of all the processes involved, as her final pieces include hand-painted florals, scans, linoprints, photographs and drawings all collaged together by hand and on the computer. She prints her designs with a digital printer using fade-resistant inks on a tearproof paper. She experimented intensively with papers and inks until she found a combination that would allow the light to filter through her patterns.

HOUSE OF CHINTZ, *COLLECTION OF LAMPSHADES.*
Caravan of Love (top) with *Buddleia of Suburbia* and *Suburban Dream*, each 23 x 30 x 30 cm (9 x 12 x 12 in.). *Photo: Hannah Nunn.*

1

2

1
HOUSE OF CHINTZ, *SUBURBAN DREAM (DETAIL).*
Handmade lampshade with original digital artwork. *Photo: Hannah Nunn.*

2
HOUSE OF CHINTZ, *SUBURBAN DREAM (PALE BLUE COLOURWAY).*
Handmade lampshade with original digital artwork, 30 x 23 cm (11¾ x 9 in.). *Photo: Hannah Nunn.*

Figuring out how to turn them into lampshades was another learning curve and she practised using lampshade-making kits and even instructional videos online. Once she was happy that they worked as designs, she sourced more suitable materials to finish her product, applying polymer lacquer to deter dust and allow them to be sponge-cleaned. The shades are finished off with a plush, co-ordinated velvet trim and given humorous titles such as *Buddleia of Suburbia* or *Caravan of Love.*

'It's funny, working with light,' says Kate. 'You think a piece is finished, but you hold it up to the light and see a whole different thing! It's contrast that I love the best, and light really brings that out.'

De Maria's

THE NETHERLANDS

'We are both fascinated with light.'

— ROOS JOOREN AND DIANA MARIA

Roos Jooren and Diana Maria met whilst studying at the Royal Academy of Art in The Hague, in the Netherlands. Roos studied photography while Diana studied fashion and textiles. After graduation in 2003, they started to share a workspace and wanted to bring both of their disciplines together. 'We are both fascinated with light,' says Roos. 'We already collected old lampshades, so we started looking for something to use both of our skills in one product.' Initial experiments consisted of projecting slides on to lampshades but step by step they found out how to make the shades themselves using their own photographs and embroidery.

The results are stunning, with each beautifully-composed photograph having a commanding presence, made stronger by the fact that a lampshade is not usually where you'd find an image like this. The embroidery adds another tactile dimension and reminds you that each piece has been carefully made by hand.

DE MARIA'S, *ROOMS*.
Exterior: photography; interior: embroidery of lines on white textile, diameter 50 cm (19¾ in.), height 52 cm (20½ in.). *Photo: Roos Jooren.*

1

They develop their ideas for photographs together and then go about searching for the right location and models. They love to find people in the places they visit in everyday life; perhaps at the coffee shop one morning, they may discover a girl with the right look for a project they are working on. They go for a natural look and like to use people just the way they are, so they rarely use make-up artists. Roos takes the photos and then together they select the best shots and decide which embroidery will fit with the photos and the concept. They have their photographs printed at an art lab on special UV-resistant fabric, and when they are happy with the print it comes back to the studio and is laid flat so that Diana can work her magic with the embroidery. After the panel has been washed and ironed to get the creases out, they hand-make the lampshades together.

De Maria's at present offer 35 lampshades in five sizes, but each one has a limited run of just 20. Each lampshade comes wrapped in a custom-made bag with a numbered certificate, so customers know they have a limited-edition piece. They have exhibitions regularly throughout Holland and sometimes in Belgium, selling to galleries such as Liefhertje en de Grote Witte Reus in The Hague, and their lampshades have been placed in magazines including *Elle Deco* in Denmark and the Netherlands and *Umagazine* in Hong Kong. The two have successfully combined their individual passions to create an interesting, artful product.

1
DE MARIA'S, *LEAVES.*
Exterior: photography; interior: embroidery of leaves on white textile, 42 x 40 x 40 cm (16½ 15¾ x 15¾ in.).
Photo: Roos Jooren.

2
DIANA AT WORK.
Photo: Roos Jooren.

3
DE MARIA'S, *RED.*
Exterior: photography; interior: embroidery of flowers on white textile, 48 x 40 x 40 cm (19 x 15¾ x 15¾ in.).
Photo: Roos Jooren.

4
DIANA (LEFT) AND ROOS (RIGHT) BETWEEN SOME OF THEIR SHADES.
Photo: Menno Bouma.

2

3

4

Helen Rawlinson

UNITED KINGDOM

'I could spend the day on the internet being inspired by all the wonderful prints and patterns, but it's often everyday things or a trip to a museum that creates a spark.'

— **HELEN RAWLINSON**

Lighting and textile designer Helen Rawlinson took a screen-printing HND at Derby University and then went on to study mixed-media textiles at the Royal College of Art. 'I had the time of my life. That's where all the making stuff began,' she says. Helen fell in love with paper making on a work placement in a textile factory in India, and for her final MA show she used this inspiration to produce a range of lamps made with handmade paper, which she screen-printed and machine-embroidered.

After university she had early success supplying The Conran Shop and the Designers Guild with cushions, lights and embroidered textile pieces. She began producing on a large scale, tapping into the very traditional industry of lampshade making to find suppliers and manufacturers and selling widely to lots of independent shops and many large, well-known stores.

Having her son a few years ago changed a lot for her, so she took a step back from the production side of things to reflect on where she wanted to take her

1

2

3

1
HELEN RAWLINSON, *PARADE LAMP.*
Drum shade and turned beech base in wenge finish, shade: 15 x 23 x 23 cm (6 x 9 x 9 in.), base: 35 x 8 x 8 cm (14 x 3 x 3 in.). *Photo: Helen Rawlinson.*

2
HELEN RAWLINSON, *BUTTERFLY GIANT SHADE IN TURQUOISE OR RASPBERRY.*
Screen-printed on to translucent laminated paper with stitched detail, bespoke-size diameter 46 cm (18 in.). *Photo: Helen Rawlinson.*

3
HELEN RAWLINSON, *TUBE LIGHT – SHAPES AND THINGS, IN WHITE*
Screen-printed on to laminated fine paper with machine-stitched detail, 30 x 13 x 13 cm (12 x 5 x 5 in.). *Photo: Helen Rawlinson.*

business. With websites such as Etsy and Big Cartel she was able to dip her toe into the world of selling directly online without having to mass-produce anything. She started making lamps again, printing them herself using all the screens she had built up over the years, and develop a new range of children's lamps.

Helen creates her patterns by working with paper and scissors to collage ideas together. By printing on to translucent papers she experiments with levels of opacity. She loves printing by hand because it makes every print unique, as does what has become her signature finish: freehand machine-stitching of tiny holes in each piece, which enables the light to shine through the pinpricks.

Most of her ideas start from repetitions found in nature and the urban landscape. She loves the graphic style of the 1930s period, right through to the 1970s, on textiles, ceramics and children's books. 'I could spend the day on the internet being inspired by all the wonderful prints and patterns, but it's often everyday things or a trip to a museum that creates a spark,' says Helen. You can see that her *Shapes and Things* design has been inspired by the inevitable scattering of small toys on her living room floor when she's at home with her small boy!

Helen's studio is in a converted chocolate factory in Stoke Newington, London, an oasis of 25 creative studios around a communal cobbled yard. She loves her studio and is at her happiest meeting her customers when the studios open to the public. 'Walking into Heal's [department store] and seeing all my lampshades lining the shelves was a fantastic feeling,' says Helen, 'but equally getting feedback from a customer saying how much they love their purchase is one of the best rewards you can get.'

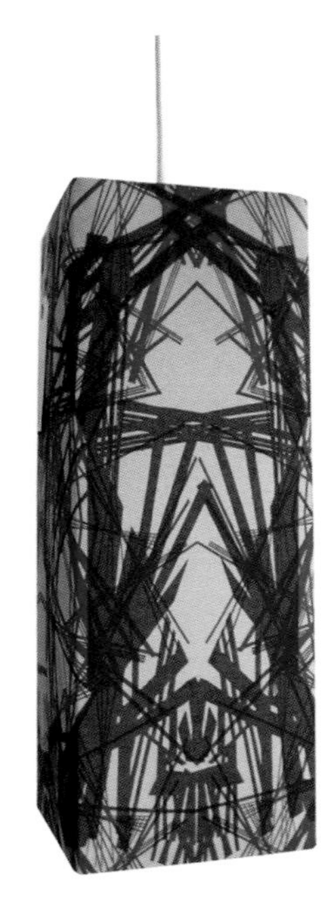

1

Laura Slater

UNITED KINGDOM

1
LAURA SLATER, *ARCHITEXTILES LAMPSHADES.*
A collection of printed lampshades from Laura's *Architextiles* collection.
Photo: courtesy of the artist.

2
LAURA SLATER, *COLLECTION OF PRINTED LAMPSHADES.*
Photo: courtesy of the artist.

Laura Slater studied textiles at Loughborough University, before going on to do an MA in mixed-media textiles at the Royal College of Art, graduating in 2007. It was during her time at the RCA that she began experimenting with constructed, embroidered and printed textiles, discovering towards the end of her course that her passion was for print, 'mainly because I love drawing and because it's the best way to get my drawings on to cloth,' she explains.

After university, she moved back to her hometown of Wakefield, found herself a studio and secured a residency at Huddersfield University, which allowed her to develop her first collection, *Architextiles*.

Laura's pieces are all screen-printed but she uses other, more immediate print methods such as monoprinting (taking single prints from ink on Perspex) or collagraph (printing from a collage) to arrive at her designs. Laura takes

2

components from her drawings and builds up textures from folded paper, wallpaper or tape, and begins to print directly on to the fabric. She works instinctively, mixing all her colours by eye and building up her print in layers until she arrives at her final design. She then scans the components into the computer, creates repeating patterns with them, and separates the colours, ready to print them on to different screens.

Lampshades seemed like a perfect place to give her prints a home. She wanted her collections to be accessible, so thought about products that would work with the prints. Lampshades brought another dimension to the work, not only in their 3D form, but also in the new life that the fabric had when it was lit. The colours changed, but more than anything she loved that the prints had a new texture. 'I print on to 100% linen, which has a visible warp and weft and, when the light comes through, it really emphasises the fact that it is a textile,' says Laura.

Laura likes to make unusual-shaped lampshades, rather than just a standard drum shape, so they may be long and thin, rectangular, triangular or hexagonal. She loves her colours to have vibrancy and an intense contrast with the cloth. 'People often think my work is about creating a vintage look, but it's not really what I was going for,' says Laura. 'It's obviously a subliminal inspiration but it's not how I think or develop ideas. I like to acknowledge the traditional but make something contemporary. Really, my work is about texture, structure and organic, handmade marks.'

Daniel O'Riordan

UNITED KINGDOM

'I believe that a craft is about the exploitation and investigation of materials and processes to create objects.'

— DANIEL O'RIORDAN

On seeing pictures of Daniel O'Riordan's lighting, you may wonder why he is featured in this chapter, as he doesn't appear to be using print as we know it. Well, this is 3D printing, a new kind of print which at first can be quite hard to believe. Daniel has created a series of striking lampshades that have harnessed the use of this technology to print, not a surface pattern, but the actual object itself.

Most 3D printers work in the same way as an ordinary inkjet printer, with the print head running backwards and forwards, but instead of laying down ink they lay down plaster and a binder, which is built up in layers to create a real three-dimensional object. It is a relatively new technology and one that is mostly used in rapid prototyping, but Daniel's interest lies in using it to produce finished objects, an approach he hopes will lead to new ways of working for studio makers in the UK, as well as the re-localising of manufacture.

Daniel starts by creating a flat pattern on the computer using CAD software, which he turns into a digital cloth. He then simulates the fabric falling on to various forms – 'Imagine a tablecloth being laid over a table,' he says – and carefully selects the result as a frame from the digital animation. He prepares the object for its function, in the case of a lamp, by adding a hole for the light fitting. Then the printer is set in motion to make his virtual form into a three-dimensional object. As this technology is still very expensive, Daniel uses a bureau service to do his printing. He has also refined his designs so that the printer uses a minimal amount of material and his pieces can be financially viable.

Once he has his object, he flocks the inside, which gives it a soft feel, adds colour and pays homage to its fabric origins. Turned on, his lights cast interesting shadowy effects on the surrounding walls, which for Daniel are as important as the objects themselves.

Daniel trained in 3D design at Bath Spa University and his MA research led him to look deeply into the use of and attitude

DANIEL O'RIORDAN, *CLOTH PENDANTS.*
3D-printed plaster polymer with fluorescent flocking, 40 x 40 x 20 cm (15¾ x 15¾ x 8 in.). *Photo: courtesy of the artist.*

towards technology in craft. 'A craft approach is not necessarily defined by the use of the hand,' says Daniel. 'I believe that a craft is about the exploitation and investigation of materials and processes to create objects. In my own practice I use new technology not as an easy option but as a way of exploring and developing my ideas and creating what was previously unobtainable.'

5 WOOD

The five designers in this chapter have all discovered, through play and experimentation with wood, how light can enhance the beautiful qualities of this material.

Wood is all around us. Its great strength and natural beauty has long been prized for creating the furniture we use and the houses we live in, but it isn't often that we see it turned into a light. Of course, it has long been a traditional material for making turned lamp bases and this chapter will show how it is still being skilfully hand-turned today. But to see it actually lit from within really is something new. If the wood is cut thinly enough the light can glow right through it, revealing its warmth, and the many variations in colour and texture of this natural material. It highlights the grain unique to each and every piece and seems to reveal the very heart of the wood.

These makers love working with such a natural material, which hasn't been through any harsh processes before it reaches them. They get to use it first. They understand that no two pieces are the same and that each tree (or chunk, plank or sheet of wood) has its own character. Light is a great way of bringing this character to life.

SARAH LOCK, *GROUP OF WOOD-TURNED LAMP BASES.* Three wooden lamps with small shelves illustrating two surface treatments: the dense, multicoloured, fine-stripe painting and the hand-painted vertical pin stripe. Average height: 40 cm (15¾ in.), diameter 18 cm (7 in.) at widest point. *Photo: courtesy of the artist.*

Jane Blease

UNITED KINGDOM

'I love how each piece has a different swirly grain and how the wood and light work so beautifully together.'

— **JANE BLEASE**

Jane Blease studied 3D design at Manchester University, where her experimentation with power tools led her to make her first lamp. She realised whilst playing with a router and cutting patterns into wood that cutting to a certain depth would make the wood thin enough for the light to penetrate. The light shining through the wood actually created the effect of light being projected on to it, so Jane decided to make some products using this idea. 'The effect was of wonder and surprise,' says Jane. 'People still wave their hands above my light box to see where the light is coming from.'

Jane's latest collection features lampshades and wall lights made from veneer, with tiny holes cut out that she hand-embroiders with different coloured threads. A lovely feature of these works is the two states they inhabit: when the light is switched off, the colour of the threads stands out; when the light is on, the threads become silhouettes and the grain of the wood shines through. If used with a clear bright bulb the holes cast beautiful circular patterns on to the surrounding walls.

Jane uses three types of veneers: ash, which glows the brightest and has a gorgeous grain; oak, which glows slightly less but has a lovely warmth; and walnut, the most popular, which doesn't let through much light but creates a bigger contrast with the light shining through the holes. She buys the veneer on huge rolls, lays it out and cuts it into lampshade-size panels.

When she first started making them, she used a pyrography pen to burn each hole by hand, which she enjoyed even though it took a long time. These days, she sets up all the tiny holes in Adobe Illustrator then hires a laser-cutting machine for a day at a time to do lots of cutting. The panels are then ready to be stitched in her rich and vibrant colours and she loves this part, as it takes her back to her formative years of stitching and making things with her grandma.

Jane has a unit at the Manchester Craft Centre and visitors to her glowing studio/shop can watch her at work and see

JANE BLEASE, *LIGHT BOXES AND LOOPY SHADES.*
These light boxes appear to be solid cubes, but once turned on, the cut pattern emanates warmly through the wood, giving the effect of a projection. Large: 40.5 x 40.5 cm (16 x 16 in.); small: 30 x 30 cm (12 x 12 in.); loopy shades: 20 x 20 x 15 cm (8 x 8 x 6 in.). *Photo: Andrew Farrington.*

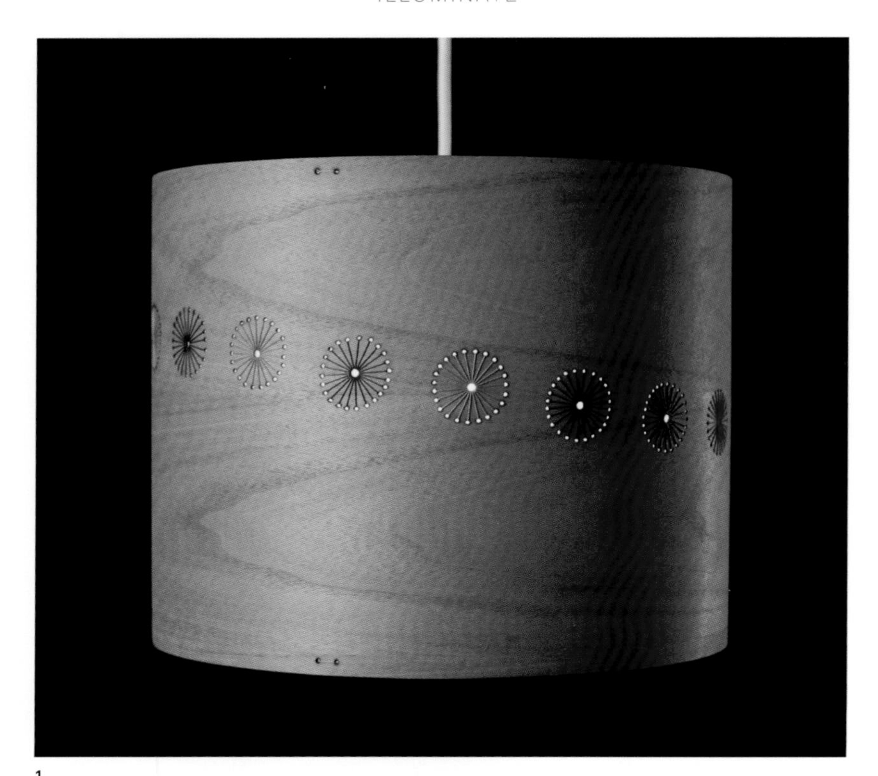

1

2

the panels being turned into lampshades as she sews and rolls the wood on to the lampshade frame – a tricky process that looks like you need more than two hands! She offers a bespoke service and likes to involve her customers in the creative process of choosing the pattern, the colour of thread and the type of wood.

Jane says that wood interests her more than any other material. 'I love the smell of it, the feel of it and the look of it,' she says. 'I love how each piece has a different swirly grain and how the wood and light work so beautifully together.'

1
JANE BLEASE, *WALNUT VENEER LAMPSHADE.*
This beautifully handcrafted lampshade incorporates laser-cut pattern and intricately hand-embroidered detail, 25.5 x 30.5 x 30.5 cm (10 x 12 x 12 in.). *Photo: Andrew Farrington.*

2
JANE BLEASE, *PLYWOOD LOOPY SHADE.*
Flat-pack plywood lampshade with an internally routed lily pattern which glows through the wood when lit, 20 x 20 x 15 cm (8 x 8 x 6 in.). *Photo: Andrew Farrington.*

TOM RAFFIELD, *BUTTERFLY PENDANT LIGHT.*
Inspired by the movement and beauty of a butterfly in full flight, the lamp's form intercepts the light, making intricate shadows and producing a stunning lighting effect, 58 x 85 x 85 cm (22¾ x 33½ x 33½ in.). *Photo: Mark Wallwork.*

Tom Raffield

UNITED KINGDOM

Furniture maker and designer Tom Raffield was first inspired to make lampshades when he saw how fantastic the light looked through the grain of the wood shavings left on his workshop floor. He based his first lamp on the form of an oak shaving and with steam-bending techniques was able to replicate the organic shape of a curled-up piece of thinly sliced oak. 'Seeing how this tactile, natural material worked with light has led me down a path which has been immensely satisfying,' says Tom.

Steam bending, which Tom learned at Falmouth School of Art, is a long-established method of manipulating wood, whereby a strip of wood is fed into a steam chamber and then slowly pulled out and bent around a former while the wood is still hot, wet and plasticised. Tom still uses this technique for many of his components, but after years of experimentation he has invented his own way of steaming 'in the bag'. This method allows him to steam only a localised section of wood and to

'I really feel the work I produce is heavily influenced by the wonderful seascape down here and the shapes and patterns associated with it.'

— **TOM RAFFIELD**

make multiple bends in the same plank. By using this method he can work the wood while it is being steamed rather than having only the short time (about 60 seconds) after it emerges from the steam chamber before the wood cools and can no longer be worked.

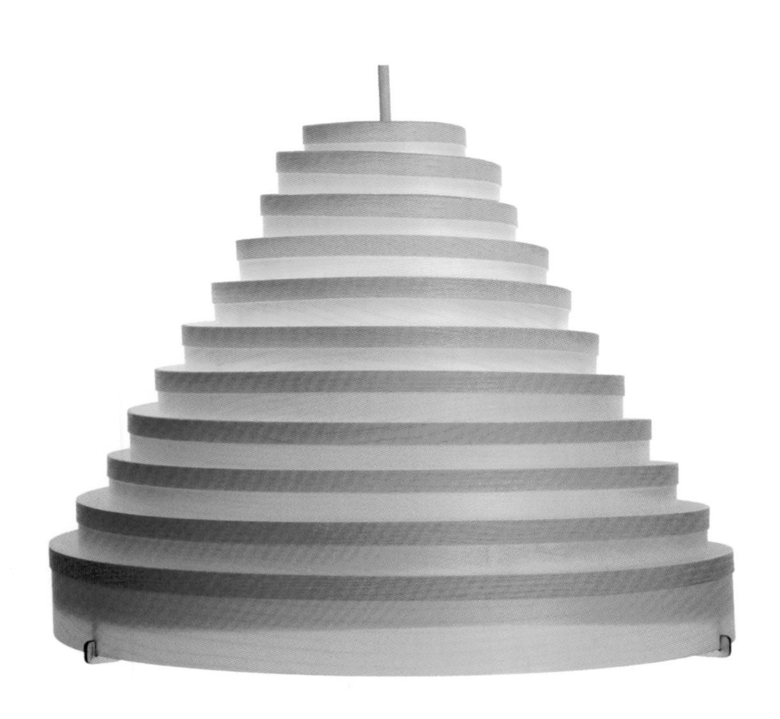

1

Having bent the wood into the desired shape, Tom sets it in a drying oven, after which the various components are assembled into a lampshade using lots of clamps. The design of the lampshade often means that minimal glue is needed because the parts hold each other firmly in place. Lastly, the piece is sanded down and finished using heat-resistant, water-based, eco-friendly varnish.

Tom's workshop is in the science room of the Old Grammar School in Redruth. With lots of natural light and old work benches he has customised it into the perfect place to work. One end has a kitchen and a small showroom. Then the further down the studio you go, the more workshop-like it becomes, with his large tools down at the far end. Tom set up his business in Cornwall because he loves the sea. 'I spend much of my spare time either walking next to it or canoeing and surfing in it,' he says. 'I really feel the work I produce is heavily influenced by the wonderful seascape down here and the shapes and patterns associated with it.'

Tom has received many design awards and been featured widely in prestigious publications, but he feels his biggest achievement is having developed his own innovative way of steam bending, allowing him to create products that were not possible before.

2

1
TOM RAFFIELD, *HIVE LIGHT.*
A tapering helix of steam-bent sycamore and ash wood suspended in place by a laser-cut birch wood frame. The spiralling form allows light to flood through the grain of the wood. FSC ash, sycamore, laser-cut birch ply, 37 x 31 x 31 cm (14½ x 12¼ x 12¼ in.). *Photo: Mark Wallwork.*

2
TOM RAFFIELD, *FLOCK WALL LIGHT.*
This light is delicately handcrafted out of steam-bent FSC Sycamore wood to create a stunning and unique lighting effect. FSC sycamore, laser-cut birch ply, 25 x 45 x 45 cm (9¾ x 17¾ x 17¾ in.). *Photo: Mark Wallwork.*

David Trubridge

NEW ZEALAND

David Trubridge studied boatbuilding in England in 1972, settling afterwards in Northumberland and teaching himself to make furniture. In 1981 he and his wife sold everything they owned to buy a yacht and together with their two sons set out on an adventure around the world. For five years they sailed through the Caribbean and the Pacific, stopping off at various islands. When their children were of school age they settled in New Zealand and David began to make furniture inspired by his travels.

His design work flourished and opened many doorways to a rich and interesting career. His award-winning furniture and lighting is exhibited around the world. He writes and lectures about sustainability in design and has set up a manufacturing workshop which is an incubator for design graduates. A deep care for the environment is at the heart of his practice. With every creation or idea, he carefully considers how to minimise its negative effect on the planet.

'Nowadays I may use a computer more than any other tool, but I can only do that because it is based on a thorough craft knowledge.'

— DAVID TRUBRIDGE

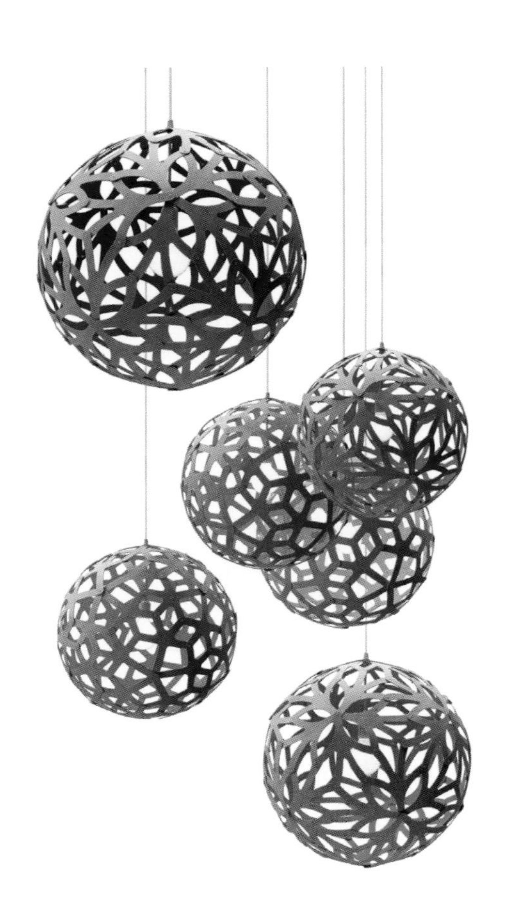

1

2

1
DAVID TRUBRIDGE, *CORAL AND FLORAL LIGHTS.*
Kitset pendant lightshades made from bamboo plywood and nylon clips, diameters 40, 60, 80 and 100 cm (15¾, 23½, 31½ and 29¼ in.).
Photo: David Trubridge.

2
DAVID TRUBRIDGE, *SOLA.*
Pendant lightshade made from hoop-pine plywood and aluminium rivets, diameter 135 cm (53 in.).
Photo: David Trubridge.

His lighting developed after playing with geometric models in his spare time, as he remembered how much he had loved doing this as a kid. He made a model that had 60 faces and reduced them to a shape he could cut with a bandsaw, but the plywood was too thick and broke when he bent it, so he abandoned the idea. Later he discovered thinner ply and it worked beautifully, so he adapted what has now become his Coral shade, put a light in it, and won a design award soon afterwards! A friend suggested he make a 'kitset' light that people could construct themselves out of multiple components, using plastic rivets. He has gone on to make over 30,000 of them. David never underestimates the value of free play in developing his designs!

The lighting he makes can be very large, but every product has been designed with a minimal use of materials. Each uses his 'seed system', whereby many small components are packed into a box ready for self-assembly. Rather than packing 'one whole tree' into a big box, you pack many tiny seeds into a small one, radically reducing freighting costs and lessening the carbon footprint. 'I have built a structure in Milan, which incorporated an integral lightshade, 2.5 m high by 2 m by 1 m (8 x 6½ x 3 ft.), with a pile of plywood pieces that I carried with me from New Zealand in a suitcase,' says David.

The designs reflect his love of nature, depicting with a simple elegance coral, snowflakes, flowers, flax and palms. Even the sun makes an appearance in his *Icarus* lampshade.

For most of his life he has been a one-man band making everything himself and it was only recently that he started employing other people and expanding his operation. A CNC router (a cutting machine controlled by a computer) creates all of their components and is now the core of their operation. 'Nowadays I may use a computer more than any other tool,' says David, 'but I can only do that because it is based on a thorough craft knowledge. You can't design what you can't make!'

Sarah Lock

UNITED KINGDOM

Brighton-based Sarah Lock makes exquisite wood-turned lamp bases, beautifully hand-painted with an array of soft colours or simply waxed to enhance the natural beauty of the grain. Sometimes she finishes them with gold leaf or wraps them with threads like a bobbin.

It all began when she wanted to make good use of some large pieces of waste timber from her partner's furniture-making business. 'They were just too good to put on the fire,' says Sarah. She taught herself to turn the chunks of oak and walnut using an old Union lathe. After a huge learning curve she discovered how much she enjoyed the craft and spent a long time refining her skills and techniques, turning out many shapes and sizes and cherry-picking her favourites to create her range. She still makes use of these waste timbers, but nowadays most of her lamps are made from lime. Its grain lends itself well to turning and allows her to bring it up to a fine finish ready for painting.

'There's no home in the gloom of winter that can't be improved by the addition of a warm glow from a lamp.'

— SARAH LOCK

1

Once the bases have been turned and sanded, she paints them while they are spinning on the lathe, drawing the thinnest paintbrush up and down the whirling wood to build up colours and create her tiny stripes. She also paints some pieces in blocks of matt colour to suit the design and shape that she has created. The bases are then waxed to a smooth finish and wired up with silk-covered retro-style flex in gold and bronze.

It's a similar story with the lampshades. After struggling to find the perfect shade to pair with her bases, she set about learning how to make her own. Sometimes she makes them from simple linen, which allows her colourful striped bases to take centre stage, but she also creates more decorative shades using old redundant ordnance survey maps or vintage silk Jacqmar scarves.

Sarah shares her lively workshop with her husband's business and hopes soon to create a shopfront area in which to display and sell her lamps. For the last seven years Sarah has been a big part of the vibrant Brighton open-house scene, where for a few weekends a year people invite artists to exhibit work in their houses and then open them to the public.

'Homes need lamps,' says Sarah. 'There's no home in the gloom of winter that can't be improved by the addition of a warm glow from a lamp.'

2

1
SARAH LOCK, *FINE-TURNED WOODEN LAMP.*
Painted in the palest airmail blue, with thin painted pin-striped lines beautifully describing the contours of the lamp. Freehand painted detail can be seen in the top section. Height of wooden base 32 cm (12½ in.), diameter at widest point 18 cm (7 in.).
Photo: courtesy of the artist.

2
SARAH LOCK, *WOODEN LAMP WITH PAINTED BASE (DETAIL).*
33 x 18 x 18 cm (13 x 7 x 7 in.).
Photo: courtesy of the artist.

Sarah Foote

UNITED STATES

'I love that the wood for the most part is an untouched material.'

— SARAH FOOTE

1
SARAH FOOTE, *SPAGHETTI LAMP*.
This lamp is made of strips of maple veneer wrapped around a wooden frame. The strips are carefully placed to create balance but look as if they were twisted up all at once, 35.5 x 30.5 x 30.5 cm (14 x 12 x 12 in.). *Photo: Kate Sears.*

2
SARAH FOOTE, *SEAWEED LAMP*.
This lamp is made in a similar way to the *Spaghetti*, with strips of maple veneer that are interlaced at the top and bottom, 40.5 x 35.5 x 35.5 cm (16 x 14 x 14 in.). *Photo: Kate Sears.*

Sarah Foote comes from a creative family. Her mum had a workshop in their basement where she made jigsaws, dolls' houses and other wooden knick-knacks. Sarah always wanted to go down there and make things too, but it was out of bounds to the kids, so she would gather up the balsa-wood scraps from her dad and brother's model-aeroplane making, go up to her room, and make things herself.

She kept her creativity to herself while she was growing up and followed a very academic path, studying linguistics at the University of California, but little sparks of ideas found her skipping classes to stay home and design things. It was something she couldn't ignore.

One day in her twenties, walking down the street in her home city of San Francisco she came across an old globe-shaped egg basket. It occurred to her that by weaving balsa-wood through this structure she could make a fantastic lamp, and after some experimenting, she was hooked! More recently she has moved from balsawood to veneer, which is stronger and keeps its shape better, but still looks lovely when lit.

She uses very sharp scissors to cut out her shapes from a large sheet; this takes patience as, if veneer is not handled properly, it can split and tear. Once she has enough of her shapes (sixty or more strips for her *Spaghetti* lamp and hundreds of wooden discs for her *Hydrangea*, pictured on p. 4), she wraps and weaves them around the frame, gluing in strategic, hidden places until the pieces are balanced around the light source. Her pieces can take between one and three days to complete. 'I love that the wood for the most part is an untouched material,' says Sarah. 'It's been cut from the tree and that's it. I'm the first person that gets a crack at making it into something. I also love picturing the tree it came from, and really putting the grain of the wood on display by lighting it up.'

Sarah now lives in Brooklyn, New York, and loves the buzz of the creative

1

2

community around her. She has a workshop in her apartment overlooking the bustling street. When she goes there to work, it feels like her own secret place, much like going up to her childhood bedroom where her creativity began.

Sarah has had plenty of media coverage, including a TV appearance on HGTV's home design show *Dear Genevieve*, but she is most proud of how far her lamps have come since the first once she made back in San Francisco. She is, of course, extremely happy when her family and friends want her work in their homes. To Sarah, these are the people whose opinions really matter.

6 METAL

You may not think that metal is the obvious choice of material for creating lights, given its dense and impenetrable qualities, but, if these very qualities are embraced, the contrast between light and dark can make for some very interesting effects.

The designers in this chapter work predominantly in metal but often use it alongside other, more translucent materials, such as ceramics, paper and glass. In these cases, the metal serves as a kind of supporting structure for the other materials, a framework that becomes an intrinsic part of the design.

In the work of these designers, copper is beaten, forged and burnished and then coupled with organic paper shades. Bronze is cast into branches, which hold delicate porcelain blossoms. Wire is extruded, twisted and brazed and used to contain fragments of glass. Sheet metal is cleverly shaped to create mechanical moving structures. All of these designers have transformed this tough, dense material into something beautiful and fascinating.

EMERALD FAERIE, *THE PANDORA.*
Light bag that also doubles as a handbag, 20 x 20 x 8 cm (8 x 8 x 3¼ in.).
Photo: Giles Angel.

1
CHRIS CAIN, *MARINE LAMP.*
Copper lamp with handmade paper shade, 56 x 49 x 25 cm (22 x 19⅓ x 10 in.).
Photo: courtesy of the artist.

2
CHRIS CAIN, *SPINNING TIN CAN LANTERN.*
This lantern is made from an old baked-bean tin. The heat from the candle makes it spin. Height 19 cm (7½ in.).
Photo: Hannah Nunn.

3
CHRIS CAIN, *TRIPOD MULTIPLE BULB LAMP.*
Multiple bulb lamp made from copper, 98 x 79 x 60 cm (38⅔ x 31 x 23⅔ in.).
Photo: courtesy of the artist.

1

2

Chris Cain

UNITED KINGDOM

Chris Cain started making lights about ten years ago when he and his partner moved to Brighton from rural Devon. Chris is a sculptor and his partner a painter, so the south coast city seemed like a good place to get their creative businesses off the ground. Having little money at the time, Chris looked around for anything he could recycle and use in his work, frequently visiting the scrapyard or finding inspiration in his recycling pile. He began experimenting with scrap copper, which he had always liked because of its warmth and also for the colourful heat marks he could create on the surface with an oxyacetylene flame. Influenced by his rural background, he was naturally drawn to curving organic shapes and began to create an array of strange and magnificent lamps, each one appearing animated

3

and creature-like. Fascinated with the mesmerising moods and atmospheres that different kinds of papers can create, he constructs a handmade paper shade to finish off his lamps.

Chris has become well-known for his rotary lamps and candle holders, which use the heat from the bulb or candle to make them spin. This began when he was experimenting with cutting out patterns from baked-bean tins with his oxyacetylene welding gear. The holes looked lovely when the candlelight shone through them. He thought to himself that the top of the tin can looked a bit like a flicker fan that you get on top of old-fashioned electric fires and he wondered if he could get the tin to spin. He sculpted fins into the top and made a spike for it to revolve on. He then lit a candle and was thrilled to watch it go round and round, making mesmerising patterns on the walls. He soon realised he could do the same thing on a larger scale and he now makes large standard lamps and table lamps with revolving paper shades.

He still finds it much more interesting to make his creations from whatever is available rather than using new materials and he carries this passion through to all areas of his life. 'You know, sometimes I forget to put my recycling out at home,' says Chris, 'but I do like the idea that I'm using stuff that people might ordinarily throw away. That's what it's all about really.'

Lightexture

UNITED STATES

Brooklyn-based Lightexture is a collaboration between partners Yael Erel, an architect, and Avner Ben Natan, a lighting designer. Together they make beautiful atmospheric lighting and installations, sometimes from readymade objects and fixtures, and sometimes new pieces from metal and ceramics.

It all began when Avner made a fun light out of a vegetable steamer as a present for Yael. When the steamer was closed, the light gently made its way through the holes, and when it was open, the light could stream out more directly: either way, it cast beautiful patterns. 'We were so enamoured with its light quality, texture and versatility that we decided to invest in developing and patenting the mechanism of this lamp,' says Avner.

They made lots of drawings, built variations in numerous materials and began to understand the mechanism in more depth. 'There are many things we discovered through the process of drawing and building,' Avner says. 'How it produces the specific light patterns through reflection and projection, the way we could control the overlap of perforations and therefore textures, and finally there was the mechanism itself. What could it do? Could we move the location of our hinges to create a ball-like shifting mechanism?'

Simple techniques are used for most of the metalwork, such as hammering of

1

1
LIGHTEXTURE, *INVOLUTION IRIS SEQUENCE.*
A hammered copper adjustable fixture – as one side opens, the other side closes, 28 x 30.5 x 30.5 cm (11 x 12 x 12 in.). *Photo: Avner Ben Natan.*

2
LIGHTEXTURE, *STEAMLIGHT MICRO LAMP.*
A small desk lamp from the *Steamlight* series incorporating a readymade vegetable steamer, 27.5–31.5 x 14 x 12 cm (10½–12½ x 5½ x 4¾ in.). *Photo: Avner Ben Natan.*

2

'We think of light as another material, an elusive one we are still trying to fully understand and control.'

— YAEL EREL AND AVNER BEN NATAN

soft metals, straightforward assemblies and some cutting. Sometimes they use workshop facilities to assist in bending and welding. They teach themselves what they need to know, deeply refining the techniques that work. They are not afraid to get help when they need it and enjoy collaborating with many other talented people.

One of their goals is to create energy-efficient lighting whilst maintaining their focus on atmospheric and spatial performance. 'We think of light as another material, an elusive one we are still trying to fully understand and control,' says Avner. Their website is full of mesmerising animations showing the lamps as they open and close, illustrating the many textural effects and qualities that each light fixture can have on its environment.

Colin Chetwood

UNITED KINGDOM

'I love being able to magically transform materials from their straight, flat, square form into something completely different, which speaks of the natural world.'

— COLIN CHETWOOD

Colin Chetwood is most renowned for his colourful flower lamps, which are statement sculptural pieces and a real celebration of art and light. The curving organic stems of his flower lamps are made from copper, with a beaten base, and adorned with large colourful flower heads, which he makes by stretching tissue paper over a wire frame. He applies lacquer mixed with coloured pigments to achieve his vibrant colours. Sometimes he makes the flower heads from beaten aluminium too, which gives a completely different effect, dramatically reflecting the light around inside the shade.

Colin is a trained blacksmith and studied fine art/sculpture at Slade School of Art, graduating in 1982. He has worked on many blacksmithing projects, creating decorative sculpture and furniture commissions, but his lamps were about making something simple, finding something he could make with less tooling. His original lighting collection inspired a lasting interest in light as a medium, and he

1

2

now experiments with many other materials to create his pieces. He makes bases from large chunks of green oak, topped with an oak-leaf-shaped paper shade, while recently, having found a passion for print, he has created his *Monolights*, making monoprints on panels of Japanese paper then laminating them on acrylic sheeting. He loves that each of these shades is unique, as every print is different.

Living in the Wye Valley in rural Herefordshire, Colin is surrounded by lush plant life, wildflowers, hedgerows and a river that snakes around the back of his village. He loves the changes in the weather and light throughout the day and he likes to look at plant forms as they change through the seasons. You can see this in the drooping snowdrops and rusty orange oak leaves that are just two of the natural forms he appropriates in his lighting designs. He works from two adjoining rooms that he built in his back garden: one room is for metal and woodwork – the messy stuff – and the other is for making the paper lampshades and photographing his work.

Colin says, 'I love being able to magically transform materials from their straight, flat, square form into something completely different, which speaks of the natural world.' That clear and simple passion is beautifully communicated in his lighting.

1
COLIN CHETWOOD, *LILY LAMPS.*
Burnished copper bases with orange and pink tissue-paper shades, height: 105 cm (41⅓ in.), flower 55 x 55 cm (21¾ x 21¾ in.) at widest point. *Photo: Hannah Nunn.*

2
COLIN CHETWOOD, *OAK LEAF LIGHT.*
Green oak base with ochre tissue-paper shade, height 100 cm (39¼ in.),widest point 60 cm (23⅔ in.). *Photo: Colin Chetwood.*

COLIN CHETWOOD, *STEEL SNOWDROP LIGHT IN CREAM.*
Green oak base with graphite waxed steel stem and a tissue-paper shade, height 200 cm (78¾ in.), flower head 32 x 80 x 80 cm (12½ x 31½ x 31½ in.). *Photo: Colin Chetwood.*

EMERALD FAERIE, *OPULENCE CHANDELIER.*
An ethereal twist on the classic empire-style chandelier, diameter 70 cm (27½ in.), height 60 cm (23½ in.).
Photo: Christoffer Rudquist.

Emerald Faerie

UNITED KINGDOM

Going to visit Fiona Gall, otherwise known as The Emerald Faerie, is an enchanting experience. The walls of her studio in the East End of London are painted a deep green, coils of metal wire adorn the walls ready to be twisted and turned into her creations, cupboards are lined with colourful glass vases waiting to be smashed and born again as caged flower lights, and drawers are crammed full of twinkling objects for weaving into her chandeliers.

Fiona loves scouring antique markets, looking for an object to spark an idea. She then incorporates her finds with wirework. First she flattens wire in a rolling mill, and then weaves and wraps many strands together around objects such as champagne glasses or jewels, sometimes leaving the objects in place and sometimes removing them to leave their impression. She uses her gas kit to braze the objects together. And although famous for her wirework, she also makes use of other materials like metallic chain, tubular glass and sheet metal. Above all, she loves to play with the effects that light can create on the surrounding surfaces and the atmosphere it can introduce to a space.

She studied craft at Hereford and her wirework began there. Although her original

1

2

1
EMERALD FAERIE, *OPULENCE CHANDELIER (DETAIL).*
An ethereal twist on the classic empire-style chandelier.
Photo: Christoffer Rudquist.

2
EMERALD FAERIE, *ICICLE.*
Three-tier chandelier, otherwise known as the Paris chandelier, inspired by a Parisian antique, 120 x 50 x 120 cm (47¼ x 19¾ x 47¼ in.). *Photo: Carlo Draisci.*

3
EMERALD FAERIE, *CINDERELLA'S REVENGE CHANDELIER.*
Cinderella's Revenge is the world's first chandelier created as an altar to the love of shoes. Floor-to-ceiling drop, 318 cm (8 ft.); fabricated crown, diameter 65 cm (25½ in.); train of heels on floor, 120 x 60 cm (47 x 23½ in.). *Photo: Fiona Gall.*

3

pieces weren't lit, she remembers always sticking a light bulb behind her work to enjoy the shadows. After she left college she began making her *Faerie Candlesticks* and *Goblets* and selling them through craft galleries. Her chandeliers developed from there.

Inspiration comes to her in many forms: nature and architecture (especially when the two are found together), botanical drawings, rose gardens, old churches and fashion. Her favourite piece to date was inspired by the iconic shoe designer Terry De Havilland. 'When I buy a new pair of shoes, I have to put them on the sideboard so I can see them,' says Fiona. 'Well, in this piece the chandelier becomes a stage for the shoes and puts them in the spotlight!' De Havilland himself made glitzy heels for her and these were incorporated, along with other details from his shoes, into the final piece, *Cinderella's Revenge*, which found a home in the shoe department of Liberty in London.

As well as her opulent chandeliers the Emerald Faerie conjures up her glamorous handbag lights from glass and wire, lingerie-inspired wall lights in the form of jewelled bras with cups that light up, and sculptural flower lights made from coloured glass vases, which grow up the walls and cast mysterious shadows. Each piece holds a magic of its own and really is like a glimpse into another world.

1

DAVID WISEMAN, *COLLAGE.*
Unique custom-made illuminated *Collage* sculpture in bronze, porcelain, crystal and steel, 114 x 152 x 152 cm (45 x 60 x 60 in.). *Photo: Sherry Griffin for R 20th Century.*

David Wiseman

UNITED STATES

'The act of flipping a switch and activating the sculpture also gives it a dynamic vitality.'

— DAVID WISEMAN

David Wiseman's work has always been about investigating 'ways of bringing nature indoors'. He creates decorative chandeliers and sculptural pieces in which bronze branches with glowing porcelain blossoms appear to grow straight out of the ceiling and walls. David delights in materials and processes and has found that casting using bronze and porcelain allows him to best express what he set out to do.

'Since a very young age I have been moved by nature and aware, for example, of the majestic presence when standing under an ancient tree,' says David. 'Working with different materials has allowed me to deepen that relationship in incredible ways. Creating porcelain and casting in metals, I've come to better understand the architecture and minutiae of flora and fauna.'

David began his casting experiments whilst studying furniture at the Rhode Island School of Design. He made casts of fallen trees to celebrate and highlight their beautiful and varied textures. When he made a ceiling installation of plaster branches and porcelain blossoms it became clear that his sculpture wanted to grow off the plane and into the space, much like a chandelier. This gave him the idea to light the flowers.

2
DAVID WISEMAN, *BRANCH SCULPTURE.*
Unique large ceiling-mounted branch, illuminated sculpture in bronze with porcelain blossoms, 161.5 x 88.9 x 63.5 cm (63½ x 35 x 25 in.). *Photo: by Myoungrae Park, courtesy of Gallery Seomi, Korea.*

David's large studio in the industrial area of Glassell Park, Los Angeles supports the many processes he loves, with a metal shop, a kiln, a plaster-casting area, polishing wheels and his ever-growing collection of casts. The space is like a giant nature table with shelves of porcelain cherry blossoms, pomegranates, lilies and magnolias, and drawers of cast bronze twigs, leaves and petals. Every time he does a new project he adds to his stockpile of trunks and branches in all shapes and sizes. Since the first experiments he has now cast over 30 species of tree. Drawing from this large collection of odds and ends is how his *Collage Chandeliers* were born.

David's work is much sought after and is now part of many private collections. He is just finishing a major, permanent, public installation of a 60-foot-tall porcelain, bronze and plaster sycamore tree for the new West Hollywood library, and is also working on several upcoming exhibitions in San Francisco, New York and Korea with his New York gallery, R 20th Century.

David loves the idea of using lighting to create an environment, a mood, or perhaps a conversation. 'The act of flipping a switch and activating the sculpture also gives it a dynamic vitality,' he says, 'as though the piece suddenly comes out of dormancy and is alive, an especially poignant transformation since my pieces were cast from nature and were once living.'

7 GLASS

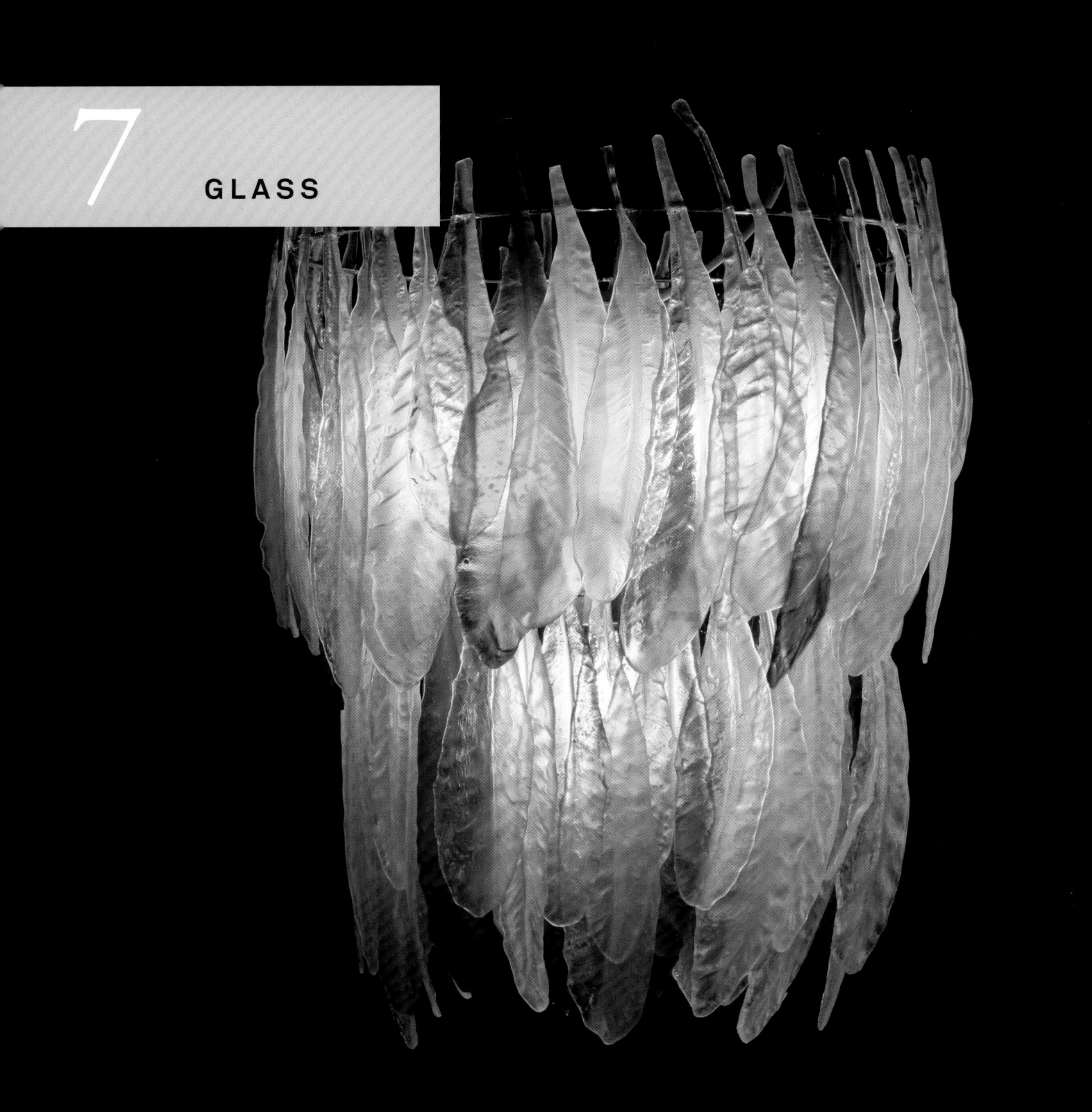

When you watch molten glass being mouth-blown and manipulated into a complex shape while it is still the consistency of runny honey, you really appreciate the skill and craftsmanship involved in creating with this medium. The designers in this chapter keep traditional skills such as free-blowing, kiln-forming and copper-wheel engraving alive, and are using them to great effect to create fresh and contemporary work. Given the techniques used, no two pieces are ever the same, and this natural variation makes for ranges that are full of character, setting the works apart from modern mass-produced glassware.

Glass is obviously a wonderful material for transmitting light, given its translucent qualities, and many stunning effects can be created. Transforming the surface texture of clear glass by engraving or sandblasting adds sparkle as the light refracts. The vibrancy of richly-coloured glass is further heightened when it is illuminated. All these designers celebrate the purity of their material and astonish us with their creations.

ALINE JOHNSON, *OWL PLUMAGE.*
Chandelier made from kiln-formed, Bullseye and float glass, individual feathers hooked on a wire frame, 50 x 40 x 40 cm (19¾ x 15¾ x 15¾ in.).
Photo: Susannah Hubert.

Aline Johnson

UNITED KINGDOM

'Every day the light is different and I want to capture that in glass.'

— **ALINE JOHNSON**

Aline Johnson's colourful studio at Cockpit Arts in London is full of her bright and uplifting creations. There are cascading chandeliers twinkling in the window light, walls filled with seaside-coloured sconces, and clusters of stripy-handkerchief table lights glowing invitingly in the corner. It's a feast for the senses.

After many years in the fashion industry Aline took a postgraduate course in glass design and found that she loved working with the material. A friend asked her to make a backlit wall panel and it was then that she saw the potential of glass and light.

Aline uses hand-rolled glass in the richest colours and casts various found objects like leaves and feathers. She makes a cast in loose plaster, meaning that every piece has a slight variation. She casts leaves in many different colours; some are left shiny and clear and some she sandblasts, creating the softest matt finish and giving an air of mystery to the material. Amongst this collection of plain leaves and feathers she will perhaps hang some stripy ones, created by fusing the thinnest glass rods on to plain glass. From all these candy-like components she creates her chandeliers. Adding light brings the final magic when all the many textures and colours are brought to life.

Trips to Dorset have provided endless inspiration as she loves the light, the fossil beaches and the seaside palette. Closer to home, walking on Hampstead Heath with her dog every morning feeds her creative spirit. 'It's the woodland,' she says, 'the light filtering through the leaf canopies or when the sun catches a new green leaf and lights it up. Every day the light is different and I want to capture that in glass.'

Aline has created many stunning pieces for private clients, her largest being a five-metre-long leaf chandelier to hang above a dining table. She often has to work at the top of scaffolding towers in grand buildings to install her work, but Aline is happiest in her studio being with her glass.

1

2

1

ALINE JOHNSON, *LARGE LEAF CANOPY CHANDELIER.*

Made in collaboration with architect David Franklin and Basic Lighting, for a Mayfair residence. Consists of 450 kiln-worked glass leaves, length 500 cm (16 ft. 5 in.) max. drop 70 cm (27½ in.). *Photo: Matthew Booth.*

2

ALINE JOHNSON, *LUCY LEAF CANOPY CHANDELIER (DETAIL).*

Chandelier consisting of 100 kiln-cast, sandblasted leaves. Drop 70 cm (27½ in.), ceiling fitting 60 x 40 cm (23½ x 15¾ in.). *Photo: Susannah Hubert.*

ALINE JOHNSON, *CANDY CHANDELIER.* Made from fused strips of sandblasted glass for hair salon Patrick Ludde in Mayfair, London, 40 x 90 cm (15¾ x 35½ in.). *Photo: Susannah Hubert.*

ROTHSCHILD & BICKERS, *VINTAGE LIGHT – STEEL.*
This flamboyant light is made from free-blown glass with a lavish cascade of fringe, 18 x 35 x 35 cm (7 x 13¾ x 13¾ in.).
Photo: Simon Camper.

Rothschild & Bickers

UNITED KINGDOM

'Light interacts with the inherent transparency of glass, allowing you to work with refraction, shadows, opacity and other qualities that are unique to the material.'

— VICTORIA ROTHSCHILD

Mark Bickers and Victoria Rothschild produce stunning glass lighting, drawing on elements from period interiors. They combine these subtle references – for example, Victoriana, Art Deco, Arts & Crafts and Oriental – with traditional techniques, producing new and contemporary designs. Sleek and simple blown-glass forms are perhaps finished off with an elaborate Victorian-style tassel or ornate metal foliage. This exciting contrast allows their work to sit as well in a period setting as it does in a modern interior.

Both makers studied ceramics and glass at the Royal College of Art and after graduating they shared a studio and collaborated on a number of projects. From the success of their first commission,

1

producing lights for the Ted Baker store in Westbourne Grove, they founded Rothschild & Bickers, creating a niche for themselves as lighting manufacturers.

Their passion is for the making itself and their pieces are all free-blown and hand-finished at their glass studio in North London, one of the few remaining glassworks in the UK. Moulds are used to shape the surface of the molten glass, which is then blown out and modelled to create the form. They did a lot of research into how glass was made throughout history and the moulds they use for the different surface finishes, along with their techniques of blowing and finishing, would have been the same in Victorian factories.

They love to develop their shapes during the making process. 'Our ideas are created, altered and refined on the end of a blowing iron,' says Victoria. 'We blow something we like the shape of and then we'll remake it and change it a little bit. That's what I love about the handmade part of it.' Once their shape has been decided, they then skillfully reproduce it in batches by hand.

Victoria and Mark have many beautiful ranges on offer and their deep understanding of glass as a material means they can work closely with many individual clients, creating bespoke lighting for shops, bars and high-end restaurants. 'Glass is often restricted to being a tabletop object when you are a designer, but once you introduce light, it adds a new dimension and scale to the material,' says Victoria. 'Light interacts with the inherent transparency of glass, allowing you to work with refraction, shadows, opacity and other qualities that are unique to the material.'

1
ROTHSCHILD & BICKERS,
FLORA PENDANT – PURPLE.
A small yet highly-decorative glass shade with ornate floral holders in the Arts and Crafts style, 22 x 18 x 18 cm (8¾ x 7 x 7 in.).
Photo: Paul Beggy.

2
ROTHSCHILD & BICKERS,
TASSEL LIGHT – RUBY.
Lights combining a contemporary free-blown form with sumptuous fabric tassel, 25 x 17 x 17 cm (9¾ x 6¾ x 6¾ in.).
Photo: Simon Camper.

3
ROTHSCHILD & BICKERS,
SPINDLE SHADE – GREY.
This range combines the rich colours of hand-blown glass with the subtle intricacy of lamp-worked borosilicate, 38 x 19 x 19 cm (15 x 7½ x 7½ in.).
Photo: Simon Camper.

2

3

Curiousa & Curiousa

UNITED KINGDOM

'Glass already has an inner vibrancy, and if you couple that with light, it seems to sing.'

— ESTHER PATTERSON

Esther Patterson, the creative mind behind Curiousa & Curiousa, produces glass table lamps and pendants, hung singly or in clusters, which are alive with colour and celebrate the simple purity of the material.

Esther ran a graphics business for years but always loved to dabble in 3D work like ceramics and textiles. She went back to university to study decorative arts at Nottingham Trent and was very happy there, relishing all the materials and the many facilities. She played with print, metal, wood, ceramics and glass. What she didn't have, though, were glass-blowing facilities, so instead she spent a lot of time using ceramics, perfecting her mould-making technique, which she discovered was a long and tricky process. She created a slip-cast table lamp with a traditional-shaped base and shade made completely out of bone china. But she always wondered how it would look in glass, so when the opportunity arose to work with a glassblower, she jumped at the chance, asking him to create the very same shapes.

1

2

She graduated in 2009 and shortly afterwards found success in the Liberty Open Call, when the store commissioned a bespoke pendant and took a range of her lamps for the lighting department. She exhibited at Tent 2010 and things really took off from there. She moved out of the small caravan studio in her garden and into new premises with a design studio, workshop and street-level showroom.

Esther's business ethos is about working with local craftspeople and keeping traditional skills alive. She is lucky that the village of Wirksworth in Derbyshire, where she lives, is full of creative people with the skills she needs and wants to support. Her glassblower is a few streets away, the man who does her ceiling roses is a short walk down the road, as are her carpenter and upholsterer for other projects. She loves working directly with clients, and her customers can choose from many sizes, shapes and

1
CURIOUSA & CURIOUSA,
STEMMED ROUND PENDANT.
A hand-blown light piece made up of two parts, the shade and the stem, in sky blue and yellow ochre, 30 x 16 x 16 cm (12 x 6¼ x 6¼ in.). *Photo: Chris Webb.*

2
CURIOUSA & CURIOUSA,
CLUSTER LIGHT.
A cluster of four teardrop shades in purple, slate grey, garnet red and yellow ochre, each shade 20 x 16 x 16 cm (8 x 6⅓ x 6⅓ in.). *Photo: Chris Webb.*

colours. Everything is made to order and, being free-blown, each piece is unique. 'I'm sure someone could make them on a production line,' says Esther 'but that's not what it's about. I want them all hand-blown, as none of them can be exactly the same.' Esther assembles each one by hand, wiring them up with beautiful fittings and complementary vintage-style twisted flex.

Esther loves the element of surprise that working with light can bring. 'You don't know how it's going to be until you plug it in,' she says. Her latest design, *Acid Drops*, is made of a semi-opaque canary-yellow glass, and when she switched it on for the first time she discovered that you couldn't see the actual bulb, just the glowing filament, creating a strange suspended loop of light. This happy accident has become her favourite thing about the piece. 'Light brings that extra dimension to the materials and an extra something to play with,' says Esther. 'Glass already has an inner vibrancy, and if you couple that with light, it seems to sing.'

CURIOUSA & CURIOUSA, *STEM CHANDELIER*.
Drop-stem chandelier using slate grey, smoked olive and Turkish blue hand-blown glass, 90 x 26 x 26 cm (35½ x 10¼ x 10¼ in.). *Photo: Chris Webb.*

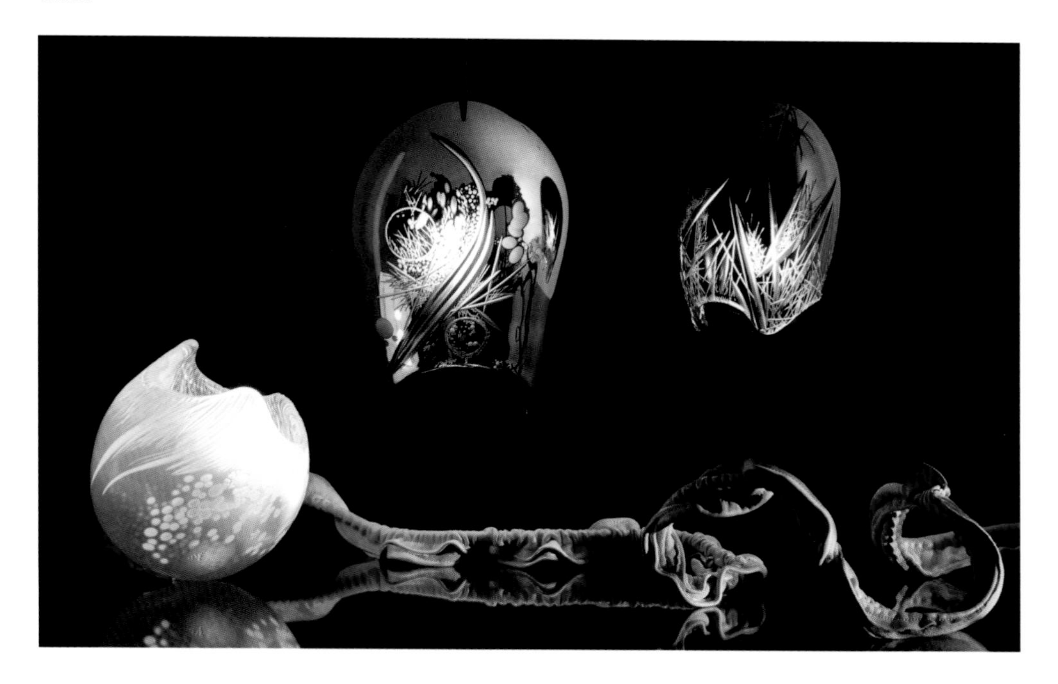

HEATHER GILLESPIE, *BREAK THE PATTERN LIGHTING.*
Cut and engraved, hand-blown, cased glass, 25 x 22 x 25 cm (9¾ x 8¾ x 9¾ in.).
Photo: Tas Kyprianou.

Heather Gillespie

UNITED KINGDOM

'Glass challenges me every day I work with it.'

— HEATHER GILLESPIE

Heather Gillespie's passion for glass began on her foundation course at university. Seeing how glass could be cut and fused together instantly captured her imagination and, when she moved on to Edinburgh College of Art, she continued to pursue her interest in this area. Whilst there, she was very inspired by a visiting glass engraver called Katherine Coleman, who came to talk about engraving glass using a copper wheel. 'As soon as I saw the images of her work, I was totally hooked on engraving and the history it holds,' says Heather. Her lecturers encouraged her to attend the International Symposium of Engraved Glass where she met many other talented engravers,

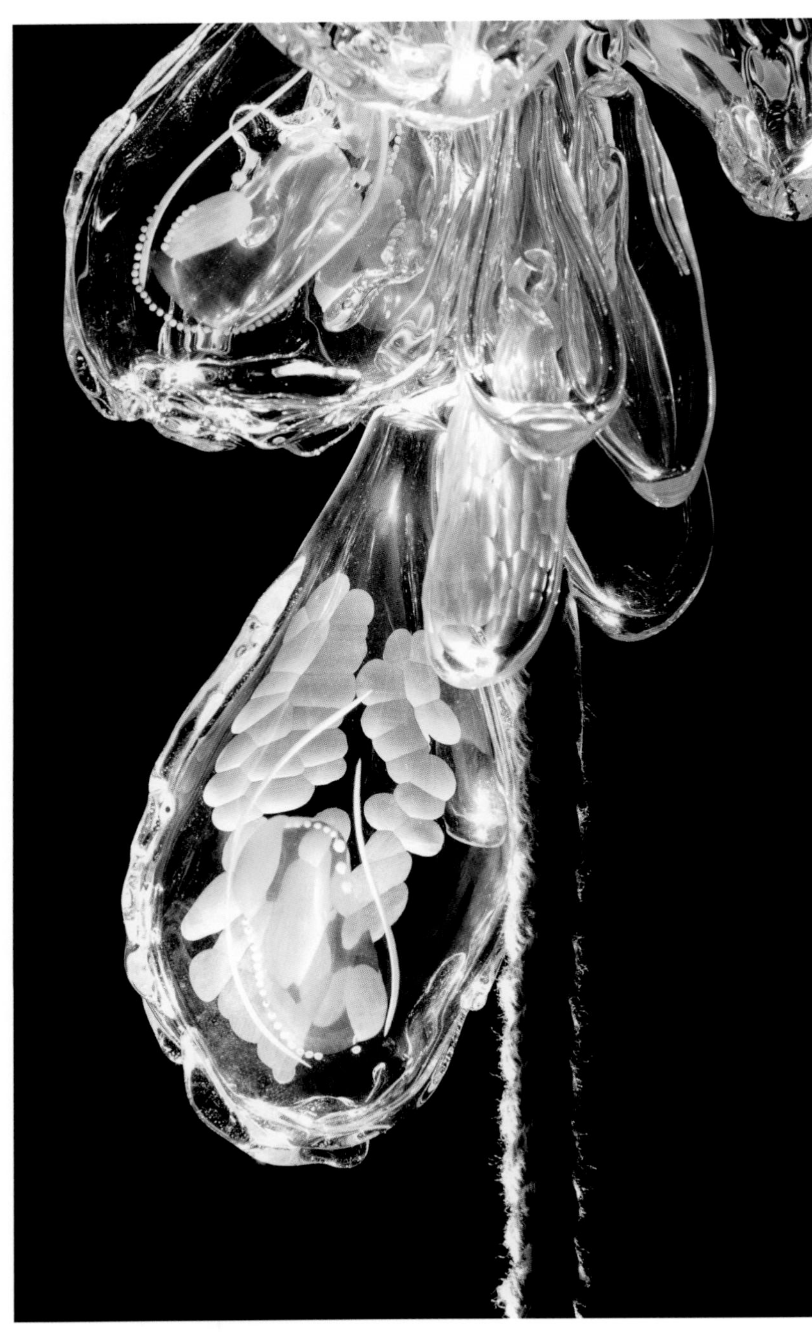

1

including Mr Peter Reth, who offered to mentor her as a copper engraver for a year in the Czech Republic after she had finished her degree. She returned to college enthused, dusted off the two copper-wheel lathes and worked her way through *The Techniques of Glass Engraving* by Peter Dreiser and Jonathan Matcham. Step by step she learned the technique; it was a laborious process, but teaching herself this way would stand her in good stead for the enjoyable but tough training to follow.

Copper-wheel engraving is a traditional technique, no longer taught in the UK, carried out on a belt-driven lathe fixed up with spindles holding rotating wheels. An abrasive powder suspended in oil is applied to the wheel and the glass is brought to the wheel to make the cut, not the other way round. It requires great skill and a steady pair of hands. As part of Heather's training, she was given an A5 sheet of glass and told to fill it with the same mark, each one needing to be the same style, size and level of polish. 'I learned patience and perfection,' she says.

Moving on to develop her own collection she began cutting and engraving vases and saw great potential for lighting. On her return to the UK, the Crafts Council supported her on the Next Move scheme, which gave her space to develop her ideas.

Heather's lathe sits happily in front of her log fire at her home in Cumbria. She has glass blown by talented craftspeople

2

in the Czech Republic and the UK. She uses a linishing machine to cut down the blown glass and then polishes it with a felt wheel until she begins to see it sparkle and gleam. She then uses a selection of diamond, stone and copper wheels for intaglio engraving. She achieves her fascinating textural effects by varying the speed, size and edge of the wheel and using different abrasives. The way she polishes certain cuts and marks gives the illusion that they are on the other side of the glass. 'It's a bit like magic,' she says.

Heather finds glass can be both very fragile and extremely robust and she finds these qualities exciting to work with. 'Glass challenges me every day I work with it,' she says. Her *Break the Pattern* collection was inspired by a trip to Iceland, and her latest collection, Rope Grown, has drawn on her visits to a mussel and oyster farm on a nature reserve close to her home, where she has been able to closely study the seven-year lifecycle of the oyster. Heather loves the sea, and the sense of openness and calm she feels living in the countryside continues to inspire her every day.

1
HEATHER GILLESPIE, *ROPE GROWN LIGHTING (DETAIL).*
Cut and engraved flame-worked, hand-blown glass. Oyster/mussel sizes: 4–10 cm (1½–4 in.) in length, 2–4 cm (¾–1½ in.) in diameter, total length 2 m (6 ft. 7 in.). *Photo: Tas Kyprianou.*

2
HEATHER GILLESPIE, *NETTING LIGHTING.*
Cut and engraved, lead-crystal, hand-blown glass. Diameter of individual spheres: small 8 cm (3¼ in.), large: 15 cm (6 in.), flex 1.5 m (4 ft. 11 in.). *Photo: Tas Kyprianou.*

Penelope Batley

UNITED KINGDOM

1

Playfulness is at the heart of Penelope Batley's work. Her oversized lighting pieces, inspired by vintage necklaces and earrings, are not only inventive and humorous but also exquisitely made. Penelope studied ceramics at Manchester and later did an MA at the Royal College of Art, where she was also encouraged to experiment with glass. She combines her extensive knowledge of both mediums in creating her *Light Humour* pieces.

Penelope's inspiration came when flicking through an old family photo album and finding a picture of herself as a two-year-old dressed up in her mum's jewellery. Seeing this small person in all the big beads and remembering how much she used to love it made her laugh out loud and gave her the idea of making her larger-than-life jewellery. A previous project – making chandeliers for fashion design label Ted Baker using recycled wine glasses, heated up and distorted – made her realise how well light animates things, especially glass, so it didn't take her long to decide to light up her necklaces and earrings.

Her *Big Bling* necklaces are constructed from many individually-made beads strung together, with some of them lit from within. She slip-casts many of them in earthenware, creating all sorts of sizes – some textured, some discs, some spheres – and then finely sands each one down using high-shine glazes so that they are as reflective as glass. She employs glassblowers to create various bead forms from her drawings and then creates the desired surface by sandblasting or diamond-cutting. The necklaces are fastened with a metal clasp, a lucky find at a yacht chandlery, who now supply her. Lighting up the glass beads suggests a glitzy decadence and bestows the finished sculptural piece with the additional function of light.

For her pendant lights she again creates glass and ceramic beads and strings them into large dangling earrings. She uses her metalworking skills to create

2

1
PENELOPE BATLEY, *CHANDELIER EARRING LIGHTS.*
Giant earring pendant lights, based on vintage jewellery, made with mouth-blown glass, scientific glass, ceramic and metal, length 80 cm (31½ in.), diameter at widest point 18 cm (7 in.).
Photo: John Simmonds.

2
PENELOPE BATLEY, *BIG BLING NECKLACE LIGHT (SILVER).*
Giant jewellery light to adorn the home. Beads from 4–22 cm diameter (1½–8¾ in.), whole work 200 cm (6 ft. 6 in.) long.
Photo: John Simmonds.

earring hooks that complete each pair. In her *Long-Neck Lights* she has used borosilicate glass, the kind used to make test tubes, which can be controlled much more precisely for a cut-glass, reflective effect.

'It's funny how I have ended up making such feminine-looking work as I've always been a bit of a tomboy,' says Penelope. 'Really, it's playing with scale that I love.'

Penelope's studio is on the top floor of an old Victorian molasses factory in Manchester with far-reaching views of the city and the surrounding hills. Her innovative lighting ideas won her the Sir Terence Conran Foundation Award in 2009. Her work has delighted the public and been featured in many publications across the globe including *Wallpaper*, *Elle Decoration* and *Vogue*.

8 RECYCLED MATERIALS

All the designers in this chapter share the same passion: they love to make use of discarded objects and materials and transform them into something new and beautiful. Their pieces are striking objects in their own right, but each one has a deeper resonance. Each of the drink bottles, net curtains, cardboard boxes, ancient sewing patterns and so on has had a previous life that's come to an end. These designers have saved them from landfill and given them another incarnation.

Whether they have been inspired primarily by a responsibility to the environment or simply moved by the object or material itself, their creations fuel an awareness of waste and recycling. For some, it has become not only what their work is about, but also what their life is about. So many products are made from virgin materials when there is in fact a wealth of materials that can be made use of, beautifully. The lighting that these designers create serves us not only aesthetically, but helps to educate us too, shining a light on the special qualities of the pre-loved and recycled.

MICHELLE BRAND, *MINI CASCADE.*
Plastic-drinks-bottle ends, reused and suspended from a clear acrylic disc, 30 x 15 x 15 cm (12 x 6 x 6 in.).
Photo: courtesy of the artist.

Graypants

UNITED STATES

'Our self-declared masters' degrees are in doing what we love.'

— **JONATHAN JUNKER AND SETH GRIZZLE**

Graypants began when Seattle-based designers Jonathan Junker and Seth Grizzle were encouraged to enter a 'design a sustainable chair' competition. They were a little disenchanted with the seemingly superficial and inauthentic buzz around sustainable design at the time, but in their own words they decided to 'get gritty with it'! They looked around their apartment to see what they could use and made the same chair out of four different materials – newspaper, cardboard, wood scraps and pallet sheets. At the last minute they decided to make a small lamp to display above each one to set them apart in the space. As it turned out, the lamps grabbed more attention than the chairs and their 'scrap lights' were born.

They begged local art galleries for exhibitions and donated to benefit events to get Graypants out there, burning the midnight oil for two years in their small urban apartment before giving up their day jobs and moving to a great live/work studio. Word spread in the community and local companies started to reach out and help, always excited that their donated waste would be turned into something new and beautiful. When a local architecture firm replaced their computers, Graypants used all the boxes to make lights and gave them one to hang in the office. A pizza place asked for lights made of pizza boxes for their restaurant. Because of this support, they now have various suppliers for all sorts of materials, mainly cardboard, but also aluminium, plastic bottles and ping-pong balls. Their goal is simply to design responsibly.

They have happily bridged the gap between hand-crafting and technology. Their shapes are designed and modelled with 3D design software and then the digital forms are sliced apart to make templates with which they laser-cut the cardboard. 'It was big day for Graypants when we got our laser-cutter,' says Jonathan. 'We named him "Jaws" right off the bat and feed him more cardboard than you could possibly imagine!' Every scrap

1

2

1
GRAYPANTS, *SCRAP LIGHT – '45 PENDANT.*
Made from a single piece of cardboard, the '45 is the most efficient scrap light to date, 20 x 20 x 18 cm (8 x 8 x 7 in.). *Photo: Jonathan Junker.*

2
GRAYPANTS, *SCRAP LIGHT – DISC PENDANT.*
Disc-shaped, repurposed cardboard pendant in Vermillion Art Gallery Wine Bar, Seattle, 30 x 61 x 61 cm (12 x 24 x 24 in.). *Photo: Jonathan Junker.*

light is then assembled by hand, with the character of each lamp lying in the hands of its creator.

Both Seth and Jonathan are truly passionate about what they do and love to see their work installed in places where it sparks conversation. Each lamp has a history of its own. Telling people, 'Your lamp used to be a Ford muffler box' is one of their favourite parts of the job. Jonathan says, 'Seth and I have always joked that scraping the change out of the couches needed to afford Jaws was our grad school. It's been the best learning experience ever! Our self-declared masters' degrees are in doing what we love. Is it really possible to be so fortunate?'

GRAYPANTS, *SCRAP LIGHT – JUPITER PENDANT.*
Spherical repurposed cardboard pendant in Graypants studio, diameter 44.5 cm (17½ in.). *Photo: Marius Nita.*

Umbu Lumière

SWITZERLAND

'Every paper tells a story, and the fact that no new trees need to be cut also is an important reason I recycle.'

— JOËLLE FABBRI

With a background in interior design and film-set decorating, Switzerland-based Joëlle Fabbri wanted to start a creative practice of her own. She first became inspired to make lights on a beach in Brazil, where a local artist had made lamps by cutting holes in dried fruits. Seeing these light up in the Brazilian sunset was spectacular! Later, whilst doing her internship on a film set in Berlin, she learned how to make paper transparent, which further inspired her.

Joëlle's first creation was a lamp for her sister's birthday, made from tissue paper and magazines that she cut into triangles. Her sister still keeps it in her bedroom all these years later.

Joëlle works with all sorts of materials which are mostly printed papers: newspaper, magazines, books, maps, sewing patterns and vintage wrapping paper. She lives in the Swiss city of Basel, which shares a border with both France and Germany, so she can enjoy scouring the lovely flea markets and junk shops of three countries. She says, 'I don't like to throw pretty things away, so I have tons of things at home waiting for a second use.' She is also fascinated with vintage items and antiques with so much history. 'Every paper tells a story, and the fact that no new trees need to be cut also is an important reason I recycle,' says Joëlle.

First she treats the paper. The process is lengthy, so she does a lot in one go. 'I love when I treat the paper and hold it up for the first time towards the light,' she says, 'I can get really excited, seeing both sides of the paper becoming one.' She cuts her carefully chosen materials and lays the pieces down on a sticky transparent foil, then sews them together line by line. After this, she sews on wire and ribbons, then fixes the lamp together using rivets and wire rods to hold the bulb.

Umbu got its name from a Brazilian citrus fruit. Joëlle loved the taste of the juice and the sound of the name and, of course, hearing it takes her back to where her lighting ideas first began.

1

2

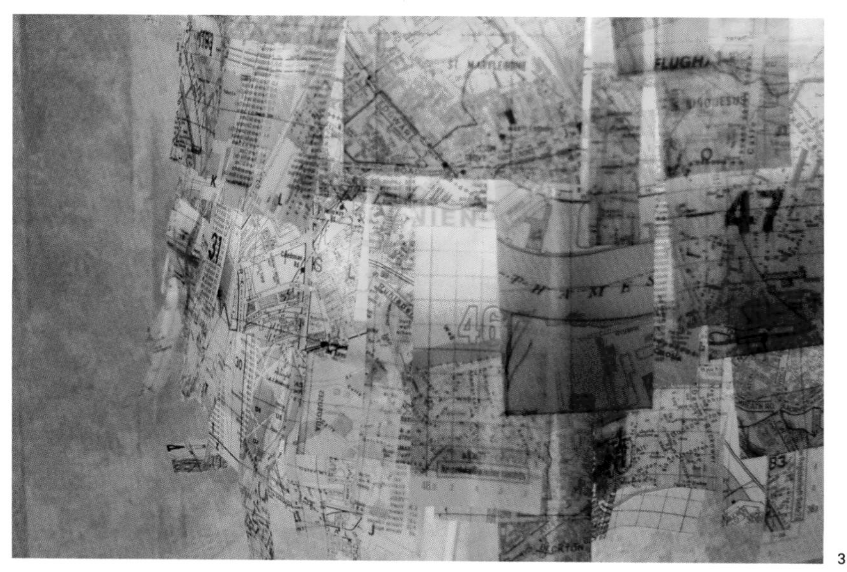

3

1
UMBU LUMIÈRE, *SEWING PAPER LAMP*.
Lampshade made from old sewing papers, 40 x 28 x 28 cm (15¾ x 11 x 11 in.).
Photo: Joëlle Fabbri.

2
UMBU LUMIÈRE, *MUSIK LAMP*.
Lampshade made from old music sheets, 28 x 28 x 28 cm (11 x 11 x 11 in.).
Photo: Joëlle Fabbri.

3
UMBU LUMIÈRE, *CITY MAP LAMP (DETAIL)*.
Lampshade made from old maps of cities, 40 x 28 x 28 cm (15¾ x 11 x 11 in.).
Photo: Joëlle Fabbri.

Lucentia

UNITED KINGDOM

It is clear that Stella Corrall, the woman behind Lucentia, thinks a lot about the environmental impact she has on the Earth and that designing responsibly is woven into her consciousness. Her passion is for recycling plastics, but she doesn't just reuse waste plastics to create a new product; she actually physically recycles the plastic herself, taking it through an intricate range of processes and creating a whole new material. The end result – a tactile, opaque plastic material with trappings of lace, fabric, coloured plastics, threads or feathers – begs to be held up to the light, so wall panels and lampshades sit amongst her range of products.

Her love of plastics began when she was studying multimedia textiles at Loughborough University, and once she began experimenting, she couldn't put them down. After university she found many helpful contacts in the plastics industry who showed her new techniques and ways of dyeing the material.

Her workshop in Glossop, Derbyshire, is jam-packed with materials she has found and kept as well as her much-loved collection of industrial machines. The recycling process begins with piles of thick, flexible vinyl sheeting collected from various local industries, saved from landfill, which she feeds into her granulating machine. This is broken down into tiny pieces, some of which are dyed. Stella has formulated a whole spectrum of beautiful colours through constant experimentation and now has a bulging sample book that she uses for reference. The coloured granules are then fed into a huge extruding machine, from which they emerge looking like colourful spaghetti.

To create the final material, chosen objects – perhaps the extruded plastic or delicate lace or feathers – are laid out in a frame. These are then sprinkled with undyed plastic granules and placed in a compression mould, which melts and flattens everything together to her desired thickness. Stella has experimented heavily

1

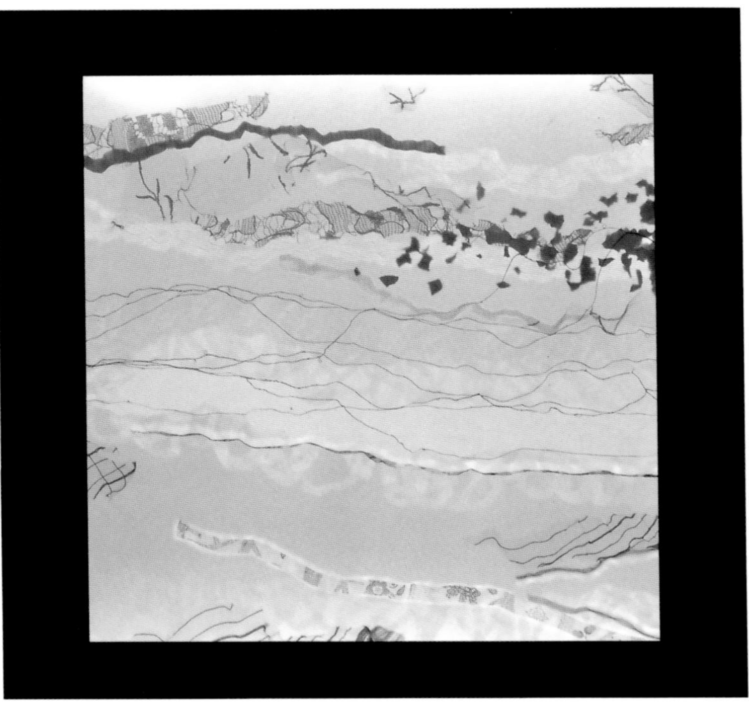

2

with this process in her quest to create a new material ready to be made into a wide array of products.

She has produced a collection of wall pieces, lit with state of the art LEDs, and a collection of lampshades made by recycling net curtains. She sews strips of the net together, mixing up the different patterns and textures. Because the sheets of lace are so large, they don't go in the compression mould; instead they go through a big roller which has had plastic granules melted on to it. She loves being able to create a new fabric in-house out of something redundant, and then a totally new product out of this fabric. 'We have created something unique with a story behind it,' she says. 'Hopefully this conversation point will help people think about the choice they have made and enjoy their product for a long time to come.'

1
LUCENTIA, *LACE DRUM SHADE (LIT).*
Pendant light created from reclaimed collaged laces, with wipeable surfaces, 25 x 25.5 x 25.5 cm (9¾ x 10 x 10 in.).
Photo: Ilian Photography.

2
LUCENTIA, *LANDSCAPE (LIT).*
Wall artwork created from recycled vinyls, fabrics and threads, with LED backlight, 30 x 30 x 1.5 cm (11¾ x 11¾ x ½ in.).
Photo: courtesy of artist.

1

Michelle Brand

UNITED KINGDOM

'It takes a plastic bottle hundreds of years to decompose on its own, even longer if it's underground.'

— MICHELLE BRAND

Michelle Brand's cascading chandeliers have a simple aesthetic beauty, their many flower shapes refracting the light and pleasing the eye. They are a stunning focal point for a tall Victorian hallway or a centrepiece above a dining table or in a living room. But look closely and you realise there is much more to it than that. Her chandeliers are made from over 300 carefully prepared plastic-bottle ends and are the result of years of research into recycling and environmental design. Every single twinkling flower is begging to tell its story.

It all started for Michelle years ago, when she was doing a BSc in design. She saw so many products being designed and sold, one after the other, and although some of them were interesting or helped us in our daily lives, their existence was not being measured in terms of their impact on the environment. 'What were these products actually made of and how were they brought together? Would our local

2

authorities soon be seeing them as waste to get rid of?' says Michelle.

She set about making something to highlight this problem in our society by taking a product that had been discarded – plastic drinks bottles – and experimenting heavily with cutting. A few of the bottle-end shapes fell on the floor and, picking them up, she saw how they caught the light. This was her 'golden wonder moment', as she puts it. She knew that she had to show the beauty of the material with light. The piece would then become a vehicle for education and awareness.

Michelle machine-cuts and hand-finishes each and every bottle end and connects them together to create her chandeliers. Her workshop, in a large room in her home, an old station master's house near Manchester, holds many containers full of these pretty flower-shaped components, ready to be strung together into the bespoke pieces she makes.

'It takes a plastic bottle hundreds of years to decompose on its own, even longer if it's underground,' says Michelle. 'People sometimes ask me how long one of my pieces will last. I say "about four hundred years – is that long enough for you?"' She laughs. 'And even after that it can be recycled!'

1
MICHELLE BRAND, *MINI CASCADE.*
Green plastic-drinks-bottle ends cascade like flowers from a clear acrylic disc, 30 x 15 x 15 cm (12 x 6 x 6 in.). *Photo: courtesy of the artist.*

2
MICHELLE BRAND, *CASCADE.*
360 reused plastic-drinks-bottle bases cascade from ceiling to floor like a waterfall, 365 x 15 x 15 cm (12 ft. x 6 in. x 6 in.). *Photo: courtesy of the artist.*

Sarah Turner

UNITED KINGDOM

Sarah Turner had the idea to make her plastic-bottle lampshades when writing her dissertation on recycling and design at Nottingham Trent University. Alarmed that, at the time of her research, only 5.5 per cent of our plastic household waste was being recycled, she thought it would be interesting and responsible to make something new from this otherwise wasted material. After much experimentation with the capabilities of the plastic, she created her first recycled lampshade, which sold at once and led her to create many more exciting designs.

Sarah has started her own 'local bottle army'. Friends and colleagues collect them for her and some local cafés now use Sarah as their main recycler. She has even been known to stop people in the street before they throw away an interesting-looking bottle!

After all the bottles have been cleaned she begins to sandblast them. This diffuses the light beautifully and is the first step in disguising the bottle's original form. Sometimes she uses their natural colours but often she dyes the plastics, creating a soft pastel palette. She then hand-cuts the bottles and individually sculpts each one to achieve decorative organic shapes, which are combined to create her eye-catching lampshades. The number of multiples dictates the name of the piece – Cola 30, Sprite 12, and so on. Each shade uses different-shaped components; her *Cola* series uses bottlenecks, *Lily* uses the main body, and her *Twitter Ball* uses bottle ends.

Sarah has exhibited across the world and won many awards and commissions for her eco-designs. One notable design is *Twitter Ball*, created to heighten the public's awareness of the vast volume of waste plastics floating in our seas. Working with design company Sennep, Sarah created a giant spherical lampshade for Cohn & Wolfe, using some 562 bottle ends, which were cleverly wired up with LEDs that responded directly to people tweeting certain words. For instance, when someone

1
SARAH TURNER, *SODA 10.*
Ten plastic fizzy water bottles were reused to create this gorgeous lamp. 34 x 34 x 45 cm (13½ x 13½ x 17¾ in.). *Photo: courtesy of the artist.*

2
SARAH TURNER, *DAISY 12.*
Table lamp handmade from a combination of waste plastic bottles and polypropylene sheet, 33.5 x 33.5 x 45 cm (13¼ x 13¼ x 17¾ in.). *Photo: courtesy of the artist.*

1

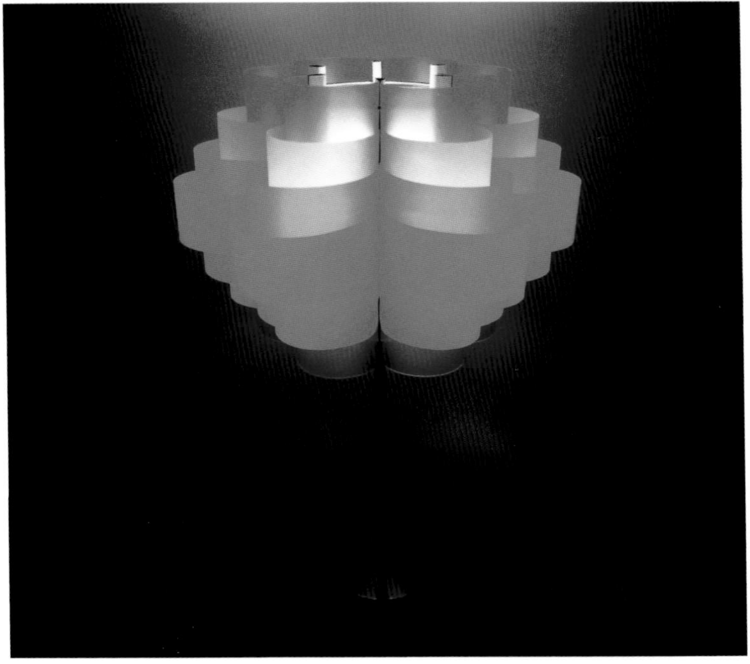

2

used the words 'plastic' or 'ocean', areas of the ball would light up with many colours, like a luminous deep-sea creature.

When Sarah switches on one of her lamps she feels a great satisfaction that she has created something beautiful from a waste product that is most commonly seen littering our streets. But she's not going to stop at bottles and has plans to move into other waste materials. One thing's for sure: she'll not have trouble getting hold of them!

GALLERY

There are so many exceptional designers working with light today that we couldn't fit everyone into the main chapters. The following gallery pages introduce some more fantastically creative makers I recommend you explore further.

1 MERYL TILL, *WINDOW TOWER LAMPS.*
Embossed porcelain lamps, 27 x 8 cm (10⅔ x 3 in.) to 41 x 10 cm (16 x 4 in.).
Photo: courtesy of the artist.

2 ANNETTE BUGANSKY, *PENDANT LIGHT SHADES.*
Textured vessels combining traditional pattern-drafting techniques and Annette's own experimental knitting, crochet and embroidery patterns, 22 x 16 x 16 cm (8⅔ x 6⅓ x 6⅓ in.).
Photo: Fotofit.

3 SARAH WALKER, *BLUEBELL TABLE LAMPS.*
Pair of reverse appliqué stitched paper drum shades on ash bases turned by Ray Key, 25 x 20 x 20 cm (10 x 8 x 8 in.).
Photo: Sarah Walker.

2

1

3

4

5

6

7

4 HAJIME DESIGN (STEPHEN GREEN AND YU ITO), *BRANCHES OF LIGHT.*
Floor lamp made from semi-translucent Japanese porcelain, 41 x 12 x 12 cm (16⅛ x 4¾ x 4¾ in.). *Photo: Stephen Green.*

5 ZIPPER 8 LIGHTING, *SPIKY WHITE PAPER PENDANT LIGHT.*
Pendant light constructed from hundreds of hand-cut white vellum paper triangles, 50.8 x 45.7 x 45.7 cm (20 x 18 x 18 in.). *Photo: the designer, Allison Patrick.*

6 MADELEINE BOULESTEIX, *JELLY BOWL LANTERN.*
Pendant light of assembled collected objects, 43 x 28 x 28 cm (17 x 11 x 11 in.). *Photo: courtesy of the artist.*

7 CJ O'NEILL, *SOLAS GOLD LEAF.*
Slip-cast bone china lights with real gold decoration, diameter 18–25 cm (7–10 in.). *Photo: courtesy of the artist.*

8

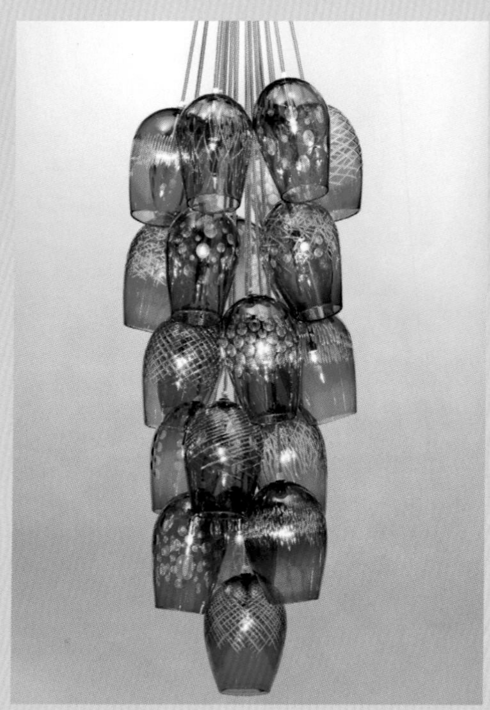

9

10

11

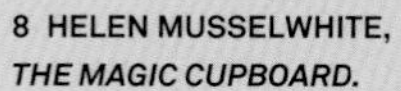

8 HELEN MUSSELWHITE, *THE MAGIC CUPBOARD.*
A wooden cupboard with a hand-cut, layered paper scene, and LED and fibre-optic lights integrated into the layers, 50 x 35 x 25 cm (19⅔ x 13¾ x 10 in.). *Photo: Simon Taylor.*

9 BOB CROOKS, *TURQUOISE CHANDELIER.*
A chandelier consisting of 24 free-blown hand-cut elements, 132 x 52 cm (52 x 20½ in.). *Photo: Ian Jackson.*

10 LILY'S LIGHTBOX COMPANY, *LOVE, DREAM, HOPE, FEEL.*
Lightbox made from upcycled period drawers and handmade image slides, 71.5 x 36 x 15 cm (28 x 14 x 6 in.). *Photo: courtesy of the artists, Felicia Strehmel.*

11 MISSPRINT, *DANDELION MOBILE SUNFLOWER YELLOW LAMPSHADE.*
Hand-printed silk lampshade, 36 x 31 x 31 cm (14 x 12¼ x 12¼ in.). *Photo: Sophie Drury.*

12 MR YEN, *ALPHABET LACE – H.*
Hand cut paper lampshade, 42 x 29.7 x 29.7 cm (16½ x 11⅔ x 11⅔ in.).
Photo: courtesy of the artist.

13 SARAH ASHE, *CATCH THE WIND, KOZO.*
Lamp made from paper and reed, 10.5 x 10.5 x 2.5 cm (27 x 27 x 6 in.).
Photo: Tad Merrick.

14 PRISCILLA JONES, *ANGEL OF TEA.*
Mixed media teapot lamp made from a wire structure incorporating ceramic doll parts, 43 x 45 x 25 cm (17 x 17¾ x 10 in.).
Photo: Hannah Nunn.

15 LUNA LIGHTING, *LARGE AND MEDIUM GLAZED SNOWBALLS.*
Stoneware spherical lights that are punched with holes, acting as a pinhole camera and casting dots of light on surrounding walls and surfaces, diameter 22–30 cm (8⅔–11¾ in.).
Photo: Joy Kahumbu.

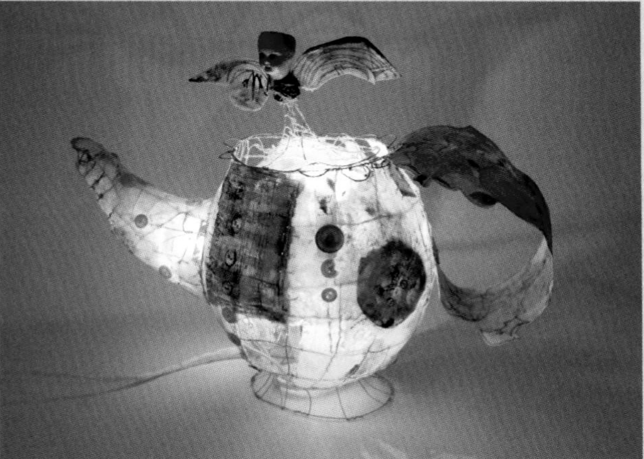

14

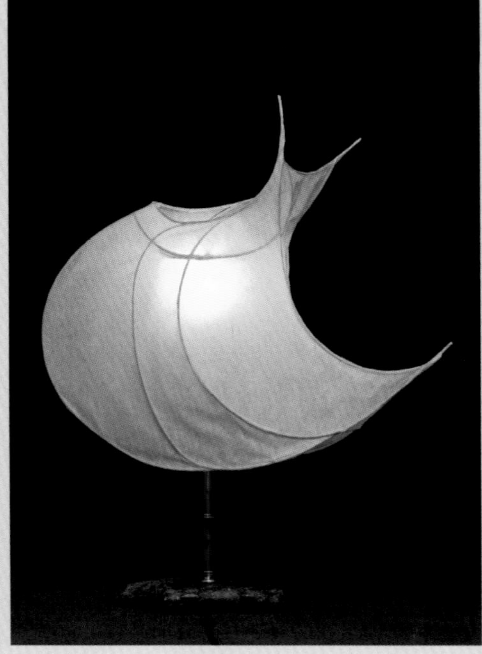

13

15

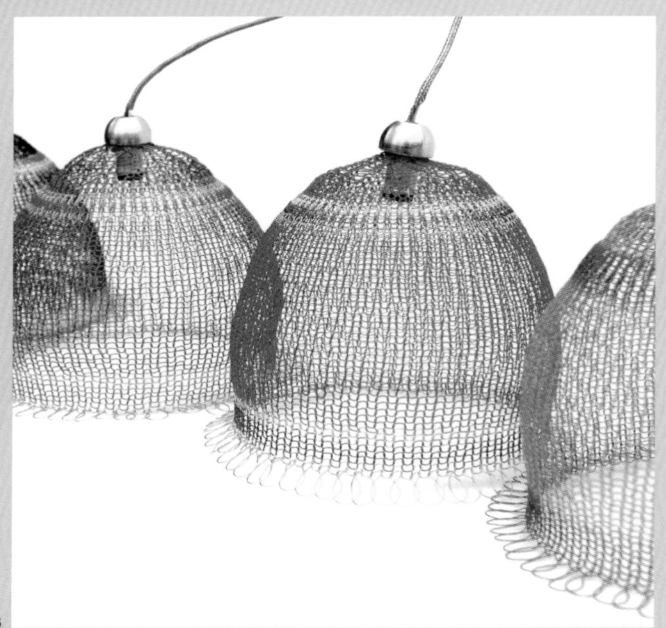

16

17

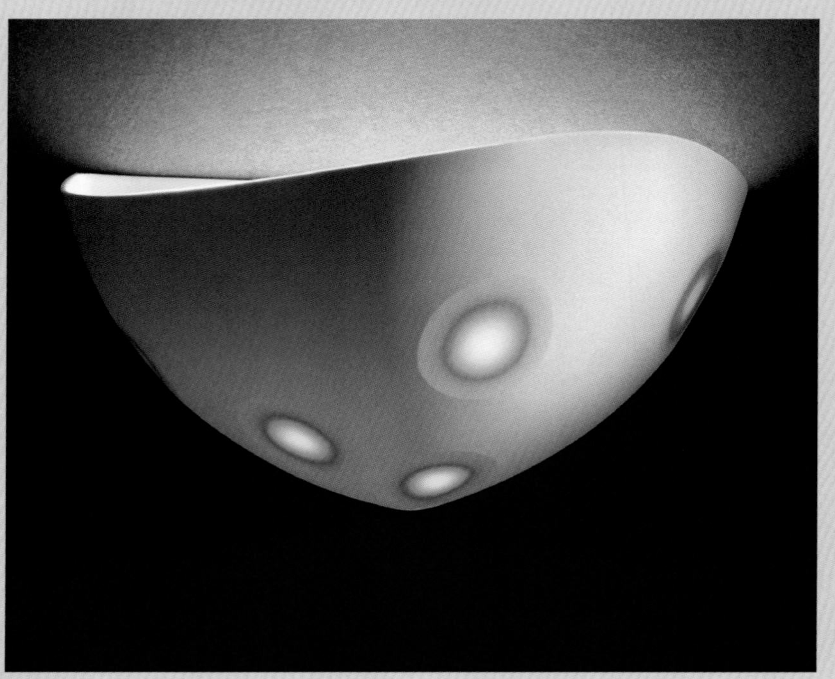

18

16 YOOLA, *FEMININE ROUND LAMPSHADES.*
Shades created using a crochet hook and fine copper wires, 10 x 10 x 10 cm (4 x 4 x 4 in.). *Photo: Yael Falk.*

17 ULRIKA JAARL, *BLOMSTER.*
ABS sphere, polypropylene flowers on fibre-optic stalks, diameter 40 cm (15¾ in.). *Photo: Ray Fowler.*

18 SASHA WARDELL, *BONE CHINA WALL LAMP.*
Slip-cast bone china, using a layering and slicing technique to reveal the underlying colours, 13.5 x 25 x 13 cm (5⅓ x 10 x 5 in.). *Photo: Steve Hook.*

19

20

19 MARIA LINTOTT, *BLOOM LIGHT.*
A fine bone china tealight holder, 14 x 7 x 7 cm (5½ x 2¾ x 2¾ in.), including base. *Photo: Maria Lintott.*

20 LIZ SCRINE, *PASSAGE LIGHT.*
A free-standing ceramic light made of a creamy coloured stoneware clay with a stony finish. A window cut into the face reveals an architectural interior. A staircase passes through successive doorways winding up towards the light until it disappears around the corner, 22.5 x 12.5 x 15 cm (9 x 5 x 6 in.). *Photo: courtesy of the artist.*

21

22

21 KARIN ERIKSSON, *SIGNE TEALIGHT HOLDER.*
Bone china tealight holder with butterfly decals, 6 x 5 x 5 cm (2.5 x 2 x 2 in.). *Photo: Eleni Caulcott.*

22 JOANNA COUPLAND, *BIRDS OF PARADISE.*
String of fairy lights with papier mâché bird shades, each approx. 15 x 15 x 8 cm (6 x 6 x 3 in.). *Photo: Hannah Nunn.*

23 KEN EARDLEY & QUINCY LAMPSHADES, *GREEN BIRD LAMP.*
Painted ceramic lampbase by Ken Eardley with a plain handmade shade made by Quincy lampshades, base: 15 x 11 x 11 cm (6 x 4⅓ x 4⅓ in.), shade: 16 x 14 x 14 cm (6⅓ x 5½ x 5½ in.). *Photo: Hannah Nunn.*

24 GILLES EICHENBAUM, GARBAGE, *PRIMADONNA.*
One of Gilles' *Lacework Lights*, named after a real women's underwear brand, 27 x 22 x 29 cm (10⅔ x 8⅔ x 11¾ in.). *Photo: courtesy of the artist.*

23

24

25 TAMMY SMITH, *OUR LADY OF THE SERPENTINE.*
This sculpture depicts a woman and her interior life, represented by a carnival ensconced within her fabric skirt, and lit from within. This piece is made from clay, wire, fabric, metal, and paint, 35.5 x 26.5 x 26.5 cm (14 x 10½ x 10½ in.). *Photo: courtesy of the artist.*

26 WENDY JUNG, *PIERCED NIGHTLIGHTS.*
Semi-porcelain tea light holders with pierced detail, 11 x 9 x 9 cm (4⅓ x 3½ x 3½ in.). *Photo: courtesy of the artist.*

25

26

27 SNOWPUPPE (NELLIANNA VAN DEN BAARD AND KENNETH VEENENBOS), *SIGNATURE ORIGAMI LAMPSHADE.*
This lampshade is folded from three pieces of parchment paper. The strong folds play with the light, casting charming shadows, 48 x 30 x 30 cm (19 x 12 x 12 in.). *Photo: Evelien Boonstoppel and Noor Vos.*

28 CELINE SABY, *RAYMONDE LAMP.*
Lamp screen-printed by hand, 40 x 13 x 13 cm (14¾ x 5 x 5 in.). *Photo: Ali Deniz Ozkan.*

29 SINEAD O'MOORE, *BURNT WHITE PORCELAIN TEA LIGHT SHELL.*
White porcelain is press-moulded by hand and then refined to a delicate finish. Copper oxide is burnt into the edge of the tea light, 4.5 x 7 x 7 cm (1¾ x 2¾ x 2¾ in.). *Photo: courtesy of the artist.*

30 OBE AND CO. DESIGN, *TIMBER LIT IN ENGLISH ELM.*
Sculptural light with inlayed translucent rings of resin. Colour adjustable via remote control, a blending of old and new techniques and materials, 27 x 20 x 5 cm (10⅔ x 8 x 2 in.). *Photo: Felicia Strehmel.*

27

28

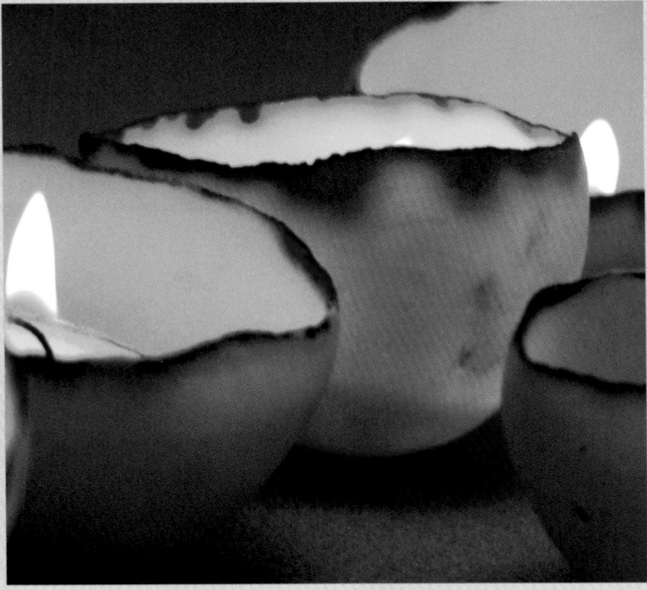
29

30

31 RACHEL HAZELL, *ORIGAMI LIGHT POETRY.*
A twenty-word 'found' poem, handmade using words from old books, which can be placed in any order on a string of fairy lights to make your own poetry, each cube 5 cm (2 in.), light string 3 m (9 ft. 10 in.). *Photo: Hannah Nunn.*

32 YU JORDY FU, *CLOUD LAMP ANGELS.*
Lampshade hand-cut from recycled paper, inspired by Jordy's architectural design for a contemporary prayer space, 32 x 32 x 32 cm (12½ x 12½ x 12½ in.). *Photo: Marques & Jordy.*

33 LAURA GARROW, *FRUITS OF THE FOREST (DETAIL).*
Back-lit paper artwork of a forest scene and fruit-rich trees, made with white pearl ink and pin holes and lit with colour-changing LEDs, detail 12 x 15 cm (4¾ x 6 in.). *Photo: courtesy of the artist.*

34 VICTORIA ROBINSON, *TEA LADY LAMPS.*
Vintage bone china tea cups and saucers turned into lamps, height 30–60 cm (12–23⅔ in.). *Photo: John Coombes.*

31

32

33

34

35

36

37

35 OSE DESIGN, *RECYCLED LINEN DIP-DYED PENDANT LAMPSHADES.*
Pendant lampshades dip-dyed in bright green and fresh pink, hand knitted from recycled linen yarn, 35 x 30 x 30 cm (13¾ x 12 x 12 in.). *Photo: Hannah Nunn.*

36 JULIE NELSON, *OBELISK AND CAPSULE.*
Table lights made from slip-cast ceramic with cut-outs, capsule 34 x 28 x 20 cm (13⅓ x 11 x 8 in.), obelisk 52 x 21 x 11 cm (20½ x 8¼ x 4⅓ in.). *Photo: courtesy of the artist.*

37 MOGWAII, *MOTH MOON LAMPSHADE.*
Moth moon lampshade in orange, 45 x 23 cm x 23 (17¾ x 9 x 9 in.). *Photo: Sarah Campbell.*

WEBSITES

AUTHOR'S WEBSITES

Radiance shop
www.radiancelighting.co.uk

Hannah's work
www.hannahnunn.co.uk

The Illuminate blog
www.weareilluminated.co.uk

CERAMICS

Liz Emtage
www.lizemtageceramics.com

Amy Cooper
www.amycooperceramics.co.uk

Holly Ross
www.hollyrossdesigns.co.uk

Scabetti
www.scabetti.co.uk

Perch!
www.perchdesign.net

TEXTILES

Maartje van den Noort
http://maartjevandennoort.nl

Isabel Stanley
www.isabelstanley.com

Ana Kraš
www.anakras.com

Maxine Sutton
www.maxinesutton.com

Ai Kawauchi
http://aikawauchi.web.fc2.com

Rachel O'Neill
www.racheloneill.com

PAPER

Céline Wright
www.celinewright.com

Louise Traill
e: louisetraill@talktalk.net

HiiH Lighting
www.hiihgallery.com

Andrew Ooi
www.andrewpjooi.com

PRINT

Lush Designs
www.lushlampshades.co.uk

House of Chintz
www.kateboyce.co.uk/houseofchintz

Helen Minns
www.helenminns.com

Laura Slater
http://lauraslater.co.uk

De Maria's
www.demarias.nl

Daniel O'Riordan
www.orchardstudio.co.uk

Helen Rawlinson
www.helenrawlinson.com

WOOD

Tom Raffield
www.tomraffield.com

Jane Blease
www.janebleasedesign.bigcartel.com

Sarah Foote
www.sarahfoote.net

David Trubridge
www.davidtrubridge.com

Sarah Lock
www.sarahlock.com

METAL

Emerald Faerie
www.emeraldfaerie.com

Colin Chetwood
www.colinchetwood.co.uk

Lightexture
www.lightexture.com

Chris Cain
e: cainlamps@yahoo.co.uk

David Wiseman
www.dwiseman.com

GLASS

Aline Johnson
www.alinejohnson.co.uk

Heather Gillespie
www.gillespieglass.co.uk

Rothschild & Bickers
www.rothschildbickers.com

Penelope Batley
www.penelopebatley.co.uk

Curiousa & Curiousa
www.curiousaandcuriousa.co.uk

RECYCLED MATERIALS

Michelle Brand
www.michellebrand.co.uk

Graypants
www.graypants.com

Sarah Turner
www.sarahturner.co.uk

Lucentia Design
www.lucentia-design.com

Umbu Lumière
www.umbu.etsy.com

GALLERY

Julie Nelson
www.julienelson.co.uk

Laura Garrow
www.lauragarrow.co.uk

Yu Jordy Fu
www.jordyfu.com

Mogwaii Design
www.mogwaiidesign.com

Ose Designs
www.osedesigns.co.uk

Rachel Hazell
www.hazelldesignsbooks.co.uk

Victoria Robinson
e: victoriarobinson@artmarkets.co.uk

Annette Bugansky
www.cockpitarts.com/designers/annette-bugansky

Hajime Design
www.hajime-design.com

Sarah Walker
www.artshades.co.uk

Zipper 8 Lighting
www.Zipper8Lighting.etsy.com

CJ O'Neill
www.cjoneill.co.uk

Helen Musselwhite
www.helenmusselwhite.com

Missprint
www.missprint.co.uk

Lilly's Lightbox Company
www.lillyslightboxcompany.com

Mr Yen
http://mr-yen.com

Priscilla Jones
www.priscillajones.co.uk

Sarah Ashe
http://sarahashe.net

Liz Scrine
www.lizscrine.co.uk

Luna Lighting
www.lunalighting.co.uk

Yoola
www.yoola.etsy.com

Mary Neeson
www.maryneesonceramics.com

Maria Lintott
www.marialintott.net

Tammy Smith
www.homemadecircus.etsy.com/shop

Ulrika Jarl
www.ulrikajarl.com

Sasha Wardell
www.sashawardell.com

Karin Eriksson
www.karineriksson.se

Joanna Coupland
e: joanna_coupland@hotmail.co.uk

Ken Eardley
e: keneardley@hotmail.com

Quincy lampshades
http://quincylampshades.wordpress.com

Meryl Till
www.meryltill.co.uk

Sinead O'Moore
http://sineadomoore.com

Wendy Jung
www.wendyjung.co.uk

Céline Saby
www.celinesaby.com

Gilles Eichenbaum
www.garbage-vpot.com

Snowpuppe
www.studiosnowpuppe.com

Obe & Co Design
www.obeandcodesign.com

Bob Crooks
www.bobcrooks.com

INDEX

3D printing 57, 72
Batley, Penelope 116–7
birch 81
blacksmithing 94
Blease, Jane 76–8
bone china 13, 18, 24, 110, 133, 136, 137, 140
Brand, Michelle 11, 119, 128–9
bronze 85, 89, 100–1
Cain, Chris 90–1
cardboard 9, 119, 120–2
ceramics 10, 12-25, 69, 89, 92, 107, 110, 116–7, 135, 138, 141
chandelier 11, 20–1, 28–9, 43, 50–1, 97–9, 100–1, 104–6, 116–7, 128–9, 134
Chetwood, Colin 94–6
CNC router 83
Cooper, Amy 14–5
copper wheel, 113, 115
Curiousa & Curiousa 2, 110–2
De Maria's 65–7
embroidery 13, 37, 40, 65–6, 132
Emerald Faerie 89, 97–9
Emtage, Liz 16–7
engraving 44, 103, 113–5
fairy lights 7, 44, 46, 50, 137, 140
floor lamp 33, 44, 133
Foote, Sarah 4, 86–7
Gillespie, Heather 113–5
glass 2, 11, 30, 49, 54, 89, 97–9, 102–17
Graypants 9, 120–2
Hiih Lights 54–5
House of Chintz 62–4
Johnson, Aline 104–6
Kawauchi, Ai 30–1
Kraš, Ana 32–3
lace 126–7, 135
laser-cutting machine 76
Lightexture 92–3
Lock, Sarah 75, 84–5
Lucentia 126–7
Lush Designs 57, 58–9
metal 28, 32, 52, 88–101, 107, 110, 116, 118, 138
Minns, Helen 60–1
monoprinting 57, 70, 95
Noort, Maartje van den 34–6
Nunn, Hannah 7, 43, 44–6
O'Neill, Rachel 28–9
O'Riordan, Daniel 72–3
oak 33, 76, 79, 84, 95, 96
Ooi, Andrew 47–9
organza 27, 30
origami 43, 47, 49, 139, 140
paper 2, 7, 11, 30, 34, 37, 52, 62, 69, 71, 89, 91, 94–5, 123, 125, 132, 133, 134, 139, 140
paper cutting 10, 43
paperclay 16
papier mâché 30, 43, 137
pendant light 2, 9, 13, 20, 22, 38, 47, 55, 73, 79, 83103, 109, 110–1, 116–7, 121–2, 127, 132, 133, 141
Perch! 20–2
photography 31, 57, 65–6, 127
plastic 31, 57, 65–6, 127, 130–1
plastic bottle 119, 120, 128–9, 130–1
porcelain 13, 14–5, 16, 89, 100–1, 132, 133, 138, 139
print 11, 18, 27, 34, 36–8, 56–73, 95, 110, 134, 139
Raffield, Tom 79–81
Rawlinson, Helen 68–9
recycled materials 11, 37, 52, 116, 118–31, 140, 141
ribbon 27, 40–1, 123
Ross, Holly 18–9
Rothschild & Bickers 107–9
Scabetti 23–5
screen-print 34, 36–8, 39, 58, 61, 68–9, 70, 139
Slater, Laura 70–1
slip-casting 21, 24, 110, 116, 133, 136, 141
Stanley, Isabel 27, 40–1
steam bending 79–81
Sutton, Maxine 37–9
sycamore 81, 101
table lamp 16, 43, 44–6, 91, 110, 131, 132
textiles 26–41, 57, 65, 68–9, 70, 110, 126, 142
Traill, Louise 50–1
Turner, Sarah 130–1
Umbu Lumiere 123–5
VELCRO® 10, 27, 28–9
veneer 76, 78, 86
wirework 97–9
Wiseman, David 100–1
wood 11, 18, 32, 44, 55, 74–87, 95, 104, 110, 120, 134
wool 32–3
Wright, Céline 52–3